Faith in Motion
BIBLE STUDY

*What If We Really
Loved Like Jesus?*

LORI JOY BELL

Copyright © 2025 by Lori Joy Bell

All rights reserved. No part of this publication may be reproduced, stored in a retrieval system, or transmitted in any form or by any means — electronic, mechanical, photocopying, recording, or otherwise — without the prior written permission of the author, except for brief quotations used in reviews, articles, or scholarly works.

Published by **Faith in Motion Outreach**

Unless otherwise noted, all Scripture quotations are taken from the Women's Devotional Bible, New International Version (NIV). Copyright © 1990 by Zondervan. Used by permission. All rights reserved worldwide.

This book is a work of Christian encouragement and personal reflection. It is not intended to replace professional advice, counseling, or medical guidance.

Cover design by **Lori Joy Bell**

Printed in the United States of America
ISBN: 978-1-969177-11-8

For permissions or inquiries, please contact:

Faith in Motion Outreach
www.faithinmotionoutreach.com

Contents

The Journey

Introduction: Welcome to the Journey 1

Week 1 – LEARN: God's Love For You 5
    Day 1 – Seen and Known by God 7
    Day 2 – Pursued and Redeemed 9
    Day 3 – Protected and Provided For 11
    Day 4 – Forgiven and Set Free 13
    Day 5 – Called His Own 15
    Day 6 – Faith in Motion Challenge 17
    Day 7 – Pause & Press On 17

Week 2 – LEAN: Loving God in Return 23
    Day 1 – Listening with a Devoted Heart 25
    Day 2 – Worship That Overflows 27
    Day 3 – Obedience That Trusts 29
    Day 4 – Prayer That Anchors 31
    Day 5 – Surrender That Strengthens 33
    Day 6 – Faith in Motion Challenge 35
    Day 7 – Pause & Press On 35

Week 3 – LET: The Heart Within Us 41
    Day 1 – Let God In 43
    Day 2 – Let Him Heal the Hidden 45
    Day 3 – Let Go of the Past 47
    Day 4 – Let His Spirit Refill You 49
    Day 5 – Let Peace Guard Your Heart 51
    Day 6 – Faith in Motion Challenge 53
    Day 7 – Pause & Press On 53

Week 4 – LIVE: Walking in Faith 59
Day 1 – Step Forward in Faith 61
Day 2 – Step Out of the Boat 63
Day 3 – Step Through the Waiting 65
Day 4 – Step with Courage 67
Day 5 – Step Into God's Strength 69
Day 6 – Faith in Motion Challenge 71
Day 7 – Pause & Press On 71

Week 5 – LIFT: Loving Others in Action 77
Day 1 – Seeing the Need 79
Day 2 – Serving with Humility 81
Day 3 – Serving the Least of These 83
Day 4 – Carrying Others to Jesus 85
Day 5 – Bearing One Another's Burdens 87
Day 6 – Faith in Motion Challenge 89
Day 7 – Pause & Press On 89

Week 6 – LIGHT: Living on Mission 95
Day 1 – Reflecting the Light of Christ 97
Day 2 – Leading Other Homes 99
Day 3 – Shining Through the Darkness 101
Day 4 – Multiplying the Mission 103
Day 5 – Finishing Faithfully 105
Day 6 – Faith in Motion Challenge 107
Day 7 – Pause & Press On 107

Conclusion: The Journey Continues 111

Faith in Motion Declaration 113

Additional Journey & Notes 114

About the Author 119

Introduction

Welcome to the Journey

Pull up a chair, friend. Let's chat for a moment before we dive in. How's your faith moving these days? Not in a guilt-heavy way, but in a heart-honest one. Is it growing, stretching, and reaching toward others in love? Or has it been quietly standing still, waiting for a fresh spark of purpose? Wherever you find yourself today, in motion or at a standstill, you're in the right place. God meets us in both.

If we really grasped how deeply, steadily, and personally God loves each of us, it would change *everything*. It would reshape how we see ourselves, transform how we walk with Him, and renew how we love people around us. That's the heartbeat of Faith in Motion.

Faith isn't just about what we believe. It's about how that belief moves through us in the way we love God wholeheartedly and let that love overflow into serving others. Sometimes that looks like bold steps of obedience, and other times it's a simple act of kindness that no one else sees. Wherever you find yourself, this is your moment to pause, reflect, and ask God how He's inviting you to put your faith in motion.

You didn't find this study by accident. I believe God's timing is always intentional. And maybe, just maybe, He's inviting you to slow down, take a deep breath, and remember what Faith in Motion really looks like.

We live in a world that never seems to stop moving—chasing the next thing, the next goal, the next fix. And honestly, it can feel like if we're not running, we're falling behind. But somewhere in all that motion, we forget the One who gave us our first breath. The One who loves us beyond measure. The One who calls us to walk with Him—step by step, heart in rhythm with His.

This is not another study to fill your notebook (though if you love color-coded notes, I'm cheering for you). It's an invitation to movement, to walk with God—not just talk about Him. To live your faith in a way that doesn't stop at belief but spills over into love for God and love for others.

Jesus said the greatest commandment is to *"Love the Lord your God with all your heart, soul, and mind,"* and the second is like it: *"Love your neighbor as yourself."*

Everything else flows from there. Faith that doesn't move toward love isn't faith that's fully alive.

Faith was never meant to sit still. It moves. It breathes. It takes shape in the small, sacred spaces of life—in the way you forgive, the way you serve, the way you extend grace, and the way you keep showing up even when you'd rather give up. It's found in the quiet "yes" when no one's watching and in the brave steps you take when you don't know what's next.

Over the next six weeks, we'll take this journey together through what I like to call **The Six Ls of Faith in Motion:**

- **Learn** – Discovering God's love for you and learning to receive it
- **Lean** – Loving God in return through worship, prayer, and surrender
- **Let** – Allowing God to heal, renew, and reshape your heart
- **Live** – Walking out your faith daily, even when the path isn't clear
- **Lift** – Turning inward transformation into outward compassion and service
- **Light** – Living on mission and shining God's love wherever you go

How This Study Works:

Each week highlights one of the Six L's with daily readings, a Faith in Motion Challenge (to live out what you've learned) and space to pause, pray, and prepare for what's next.

Each week builds on the one before, helping you move from simply knowing about God to walking closely with Him—in step, in trust, and in love. You'll meet real people in Scripture who encountered God in the middle of their mess and discovered that His love was already moving toward them. Just like it's moving toward you.

Whether you're reading this alone with a glass of sweet tea (my preferred beverage) or gathered with a small group (and maybe someone brought snacks—bless them), my prayer is that what begins here doesn't stay on these pages. I pray it moves into your thoughts, your choices, your relationships, and your everyday life.

My friend, take a deep breath, open your heart, and get ready to move. Because when faith moves, love shows. And **when love shows, the world sees Jesus.** Let's begin this journey together—one step, one act of love, one moment of faith at a time.

Week 1

LEARN

God's Love For You

Week 1 — Introduction
LEARN: God's Love For You

Let love be the foundation. You can't give what you haven't received.

Before we can walk in love, we've got to **learn** what real love looks like. Not the kind that fades when we fail or depends on what we bring to the table, but the kind that stays—the kind that steps right into our mess, knows us by name, and refuses to let go. And let's be honest—sometimes we're better at talking about love than actually letting God love us first. But this week is about slowing down long enough to receive it—to stop performing, stop fixing, and simply be loved.

God's love isn't distant or abstract. It's close. It's steady. It's kind. It's the love that calls you His. The same love that sent Jesus to the cross, not out of duty, but out of delight, to bring you home to His heart. It's not the Sunday-school answer or the idea of love we recite—it's the real thing. And until you know how deeply you're loved, it's hard to live it out or share it with anyone else.

So as you step into this first week, remember: you're not working for God's love. You're walking from it. His love shapes your **identity**. This kind of love doesn't just comfort you; it begins to transform you, reminding you who you are and Whose you are. His love is where this journey begins.

And let it be a week of remembering what's always been true: you are seen, you are known, and you are loved—completely, unconditionally, right here and right now. As you learn His love, let it begin shaping how you live it. The more you understand His heart for you, the more freely you'll lean into loving Him back.

This week you'll explore:

- How God **sees** you
- The **pursuing** heart of God
- His faithful **protection** and **provision**
- The power of **forgiveness**
- The **steadfast love** that calls you His

You can't pour out what you don't have. So before you move or strive, pause. Let His love wash over you until it becomes the beat of your steps.

 LEARN　　　　　　　　　　　　　Week 1 – Day 1

Seen and Known by God

Scripture

Genesis 16:13 — She gave this name to the Lord who spoke to her: "You are the God who sees me," for she said, "I have now seen the One who sees me."

Read: Genesis 16:7–13

Truth: God's love notices the overlooked and finds you in hidden places.

Are there days when you feel invisible? I can tell you, I've had those days. We keep showing up, doing what needs to be done, but deep down we wonder if anyone really sees how hard it is. We might smile and keep moving, but inside, we're running on empty.

I still remember a moment years ago when I was folding laundry late at night, everyone asleep, dishes in the sink, and tears quietly rolling down my cheeks. Nothing dramatic had happened—just the quiet ache of feeling unseen. The kind where you do all the things, show up for everyone, and still wonder if anyone really notices. I remember staring at that never-ending pile of socks and thinking, *"Lord, if You can multiply loaves and fish, surely You can help me find matching pairs."*

That's exactly where Hagar found herself. Not in a laundry room, but in her own kind of desert. She wasn't powerful or admired. She was a servant caught in someone else's plan. Used, mistreated, and then sent away when things became complicated. Pregnant, scared, and alone, she ran into the wilderness with no plan and no direction. The desert stretched endlessly before her, and I imagine her wondering, Does anyone even care where I end up?

But God found her there. He didn't wait for her to find Him first. He came to her—right in the middle of nowhere. He called her by name, something no one else had done. He saw her pain and her story, and He offered not judgment but compassion. He reminded her that her life still had purpose and her child still had promise. In awe, Hagar whispered the name that still echoes through time: *"You are the God who sees me."*

That name, El Roi, means "the God who sees." But it's not just that He sees what you're going through—He sees **you**. He notices the details no one else does. His gaze isn't casual or distant; it's loving and intentional. He's not watching from afar. He's drawing near with care.

And He still sees. He sees you when you're tired and holding everything together. He sees your effort, your faithfulness, and your quiet perseverance when it feels like no one else does.

A friend once told me about a man in his church who'd been out of work for months. Every morning, he'd still get up early, shave, dress for work, and walk around the block before returning home to search for jobs. When asked why he did it, he said, *"Because I need to remind myself that God still sees me, even when the world doesn't."*

That simple faith, that quiet confidence in being seen, is what Hagar discovered in the desert. It's what keeps us steady when life feels uncertain. The same God who saw her sees us today, right here and right now, wherever we are.

Friend, maybe today feels like that wilderness. Maybe you're wondering if anyone notices your struggle or the effort it takes just to keep going. Be assured that **God sees you**. Not just your situation, but **you**.

If I could look you in the eyes right now, I'd tell you this: You are not invisible! God sees you. He knows your name, your struggle, your story, and He hasn't lost sight of you for a single moment.

Pray

El Roi, thank You for seeing me in the moments when I feel unseen. Thank You for knowing my name, my story, and my heart. Help me rest in the truth that Your eyes are always on me and Your love never looks away. Amen.

Reflect

What one truth or moment from today's reading stood out to you?

_____

_____

 LEARN   Week 1 – Day 2

Pursued and Redeemed

Scripture

John 4:10 — Jesus answered her, "If you knew the gift of God and who it is that asks you for a drink, you would have asked him and he would have given you living water."

Read: John 4:1-26

Truth: God's love comes looking for you and restores what's broken.

Have you ever felt unwanted? Like no matter how hard you try, you somehow fall short of what others expect or what you wish you could be? That's where we meet a woman carrying more than a water jar. And let's be honest, we've all carried more than our share to the well some days—water, worry, and maybe a little attitude too.

She came seeking water, not worth. But Jesus was waiting to give her both. The walk to the well was long, the sun was hot, and her heart was tired. She came alone, carrying her water jar and a lifetime of disappointment.

This broken woman wasn't immoral or wild the way she's often portrayed. In her culture, women couldn't choose divorce. Only men could. So if she'd been married several times, it likely meant she'd been abandoned several times. It's even possible that she couldn't have children, and in that world, infertility was seen as a curse. She was probably left, again and again, not because of who she was, but because of what she couldn't give.

Imagine the sting of that. The many whispers. The constant rejection. The ache of feeling unworthy, unseen, and unloved. And yet, Jesus went out of His way to meet her. He didn't have to travel through Samaria. Most Jews avoided that route entirely. But Jesus "had to" go, Scripture says because she was there.

He didn't start with condemnation or correction. He started with compassion. *"Will you give Me a drink?"* he asked. Simple words, but they broke centuries of social and religious barriers. A Jewish man wasn't supposed to talk to a Samaritan woman, but love isn't limited by rules or reputation.

When Jesus revealed that He knew her story—every failed relationship, every silent wound—she must have held her breath, waiting for the judgment and rejection that never came. Instead, He offered her living water. Acceptance. Restoration. Hope. He saw what no one else had ever seen: her worth.

That day, everything changed. The woman who came to the well hiding from people left running toward them, shouting, *"Come see a man who told me everything I ever did — and loved me anyway!"* That's redemption, friend! God's love doesn't just find you; it pursues you. Even when you're avoiding eye contact, hiding your hurt, or carrying shame that's not yours to bear.

I once talked with a man who felt completely undone after his wife's affair. He said the hardest part wasn't the betrayal. It was believing he wasn't worth staying for. For months, he carried that ache like a shadow until one night, sitting alone, he prayed, *"God, if You still see me, I need You to show me."* And in that quiet moment, he sensed it deep in his spirit: *"I still see you. I still love you."* It didn't erase the pain, but it began to heal the lie that he wasn't enough.

That's what Jesus does. He meets us in our isolation and turns our emptiness into overflow. Maybe today, you're standing at your own "well"—weary, uncertain, wondering if God really cares. Friend, He does. He hasn't stopped pursuing you. He sees every wound, every rejection, every hidden ache.

If I were sitting with you right now, I'd lean in and say this: You are not beyond His reach. You are not too far gone. The same Savior who went out of His way to meet one broken-hearted woman in Samaria is coming for you too—not to condemn, but to redeem.

Pray

Jesus, thank You for pursuing me when I feel forgotten. Thank You for seeing beyond my failures and wounds, and for offering living water that never runs dry. Heal the places where rejection has taken root and remind me that Your love always comes looking for me. Amen.

Reflect

What one truth or moment from today's reading stood out to you?

 **LEARN** Week 1 – Day 3

Protected and Provided For

Scripture

1 Kings 17:14 — For this is what the Lord, the God of Israel, says: "The jar of flour will not be used up and the jug of oil will not run dry until the day the Lord sends rain on the land."

Read: 1 Kings 17:7-16

Truth: God's love safeguards your life and supplies your needs.

Faith often grows in the tension between not enough and just enough. Have you ever been in a season like this where you didn't know how things were going to work out? When what you had in your hands just didn't seem like enough? That's where we find the widow of Zarephath.

She was down to her last handful of flour and a little oil. Just enough to make one small meal for herself and her son before facing starvation. And right at that moment, God sent a prophet named Elijah to her door asking her to share what little she had left.

It doesn't make sense, does it? Why would God ask her to give when she was running on empty? But sometimes, the miracle doesn't come after we have plenty—it comes when we trust Him with our not-enough.

Elijah didn't just ask her for bread; he brought her a promise. *"Don't be afraid,"* he said. *"The jar of flour will not be used up and the jug of oil will not run dry."* And as she stepped out in faith, that promise became her provision. Every day, there was just enough. Not too much, not too little. Just enough to remind her that God hadn't forgotten her.

That's the kind of love that protects and provides. It watches over us when we're worn and whispers, *"I will take care of you."* Even when the cupboards look bare or the answers haven't come, His presence becomes the provision. His peace fills the spaces that fear once held.

I think about a single dad I once knew who worked long hours trying to keep things together for his kids. There were nights he'd sit at the kitchen table with bills spread out in front of him, wondering how to stretch what little he had. He told me once that he started praying over his empty wallet—not for money, but for peace. And over time, he saw quiet provision show up in small ways: an unexpected check, a friend bringing groceries, a neighbor mowing the lawn without being asked.

Friend, God kept refilling his jar! That's how God works. Sometimes it's not the kind of refill we expect. He may skip the fancy blessings and go straight for the practical kind, like full gas tanks, quiet peace, and found socks. His provision often shows up quietly. Not as overflowing abundance, but as daily faithfulness. Just enough strength for today. Just enough grace for this moment. Just enough love to keep you going.

Maybe today you're standing in your own kitchen of not-enough. Not enough money, energy, answers, or hope. But the same God who kept the widow's jar from running dry is watching over you, too. He sees the bills on the counter, the prayers whispered in the quiet, the weight you're carrying that no one else knows about. And right there, in the middle of the ordinary, He's already working. The oil is still flowing, even if you can't see it yet.

When tomorrow feels uncertain, let this truth steady you: God's love never runs dry. The same God who provided then is providing now—for you, right here, today. God's love is not just distant comfort; it's daily provision. It will meet you right where you are and give you exactly what you need for today.

Pray

Jehovah Jireh, my Provider, thank You for seeing my needs and meeting them in ways I sometimes overlook. Teach me to trust You with the little I have, believing You can make it enough. Fill my heart with peace as I rest in Your faithful care. Amen.

Reflect

What one truth or moment from today's reading stood out to you?

_____

_____

 LEARN   Week 1 – Day 4

Forgiven and Set Free

Scripture

John 8:10–11 — Jesus straightened up and asked her, "Woman, where are they? Has no one condemned you?" "No one, sir," she said. "Then neither do I condemn you," Jesus declared. "Go now and leave your life of sin."

Read: John 8:1–11

Truth: God's love offers grace, not condemnation, freeing you from shame and giving you a new start.

Shame is heavy, isn't it? It doesn't always come from headline sins. Sometimes it hides in the small things—the careless words, the quick judgments, or that one moment you wish you could edit out like a bad selfie. It sits quietly in your heart, whispering that what you've done defines who you are.

It tells you you've gone too far, that you should've known better, that God could never really forget what you can't stop remembering. It's that sinking feeling when you realize you've wounded someone and can't undo it—the weight that makes you replay conversations, rewrite endings, and whisper, "How could I have said that?"

That's where we find the woman caught in adultery. Dragged through the streets by religious leaders, she stood humiliated in front of a crowd ready to stone her. They didn't see a person; they saw a problem. She was nothing more than a pawn in their plan to trap Jesus. Her worst moment had been dragged into public view, and she braced herself for the first stone to fall.

But Jesus didn't condemn her. He knelt down and began to write in the dust. Scripture doesn't tell us what He wrote, but I like to think He was drawing attention away from her giving her dignity while the angry voices around her quieted. Then He stood and said the words that shifted everything: *"Let the one without sin throw the first stone."* One by one, the stones dropped, the accusers left, and she was there alone with the only One truly qualified to judge her.

He looked at her, not with disgust but with compassion, and said, *"Where are they? Has no one condemned you?"* When she answered, *"No one, Lord,"* He spoke freedom: *"Then neither do I condemn you."* In a single breath, the weight of her shame met the warmth of His mercy—and everything changed. That's the heart of God's forgiveness. It overcomes sin with love. It doesn't erase the past; it redeems it. His mercy restores what shame tried to bury.

I'll never forget the time I had to face my own moment of regret and shame. Years ago, I got caught up in a conversation that turned into gossip. I didn't mean for it to go so far, but it did—and it deeply hurt someone. In the fallout, that person even lost her job. I felt sick with guilt. I wanted to hide, to undo it, to somehow make it disappear. For months, I carried that shame, convinced that one mistake had ruined my witness and my worth.

But slowly, through prayer and repentance, God began to meet me in that place of regret. Not with condemnation, but with grace. He didn't excuse what I had done, but He reminded me that His forgiveness wasn't just for "bigger sins." It was for mine too. He showed me that mercy restores sin and sinner.

That's the power of His love. Jesus doesn't just forgive; He restores. He steps into the very places where we feel disqualified and whispers, *"You're still Mine. Let's start again."*

Friend, maybe you know what it's like to live with that kind of guilt. The kind that sits heavy, whispering that you should've known better. But Jesus says, *"Neither do I condemn you."* His grace doesn't deny the truth. It redeems it. You don't have to keep carrying what He already carried to the cross. Let grace do what guilt never could. You are forgiven, seen, and still chosen by the One who calls you His own.

Pray

Jesus, thank You for seeing me with compassion instead of condemnation. Thank You for trading my shame for Your mercy and my guilt for Your grace. Help me to walk in that forgiveness and extend it freely to others. Amen.

Reflect

What one truth or moment from today's reading stood out to you?

 **LEARN**   Week 1 – Day 5

Called His Own

Scripture

Romans 8:38–39 — For I am convinced that neither death nor life, neither angels nor demons, neither the present nor the future, nor any powers, neither height nor depth, nor anything else in all creation, will be able to separate us from the love of God that is in Christ Jesus our Lord.

Read: John 17:20–26 and Romans 8:31–39

Truth: God's love is forever and personal. Nothing can separate you from His heart.

There's something almost breathtaking about realizing that Jesus prayed for you. On the night before His crucifixion—when His closest friends were about to scatter and the weight of the cross loomed heavy—He lifted His eyes to heaven and began to pray. He could have asked for strength to endure what was coming, or for His suffering to pass. Instead, He prayed for people who weren't even there yet. He prayed for you and me.

I don't know about you, but that truth still stops me in my tracks. Out of everything He could have focused on, His heart turned toward us. *"Father,"* He said, *"I pray for those who will believe in Me."*

That one sentence reaches across time and touches every believer who would ever call His name—every future disciple, every weary heart still finding its way home. In His final hours, when most would have been consumed with fear or pain, Jesus wasn't thinking of escape; He was thinking of love. He was thinking of you and me.

In that prayer, He asked the Father to let you know the same love that He Himself had known since before the world began—a love unshakable and eternal, a love that doesn't waver with emotion or depend on performance. It's a love that never quits, never fades, never lets go. That's the love that defines you.

But if you're anything like me, it's a truth you can nod along to yet struggle to truly believe. Because life has a way of making us question love. We stumble, we drift, we fail, and somewhere in the noise, we start to wonder, Could God really still love me after that? Maybe after the harsh words we wish we could take back. The season we went silent on prayer. The months that felt more like surviving than believing.

Paul must have known how easily we forget, because in Romans 8 he doesn't whisper about God's love—he declares it. He stacks up every possible threat—death, life, angels, demons, fear, the future—and sweeps them aside with one unshakable truth: nothing can separate you from the love of God. Nothing. Not your past, not your doubts, not your mistakes, not even the distance you feel right now. His love doesn't loosen its grip when yours does.

I remember talking once with a friend who had quietly drifted from her faith. "*I think God's moved on,*" she said. "*It's been years since I've prayed. I don't even know where to start.*" I told her, "*If His love could be lost, He would've let go of me a long time ago—but He hasn't.*" Tears filled her eyes, and I could almost see the moment hope returned. For the first time in years, she believed that God's love isn't earned or lost; it simply is.

That's the kind of love Jesus prayed you would know. The love that holds when everything else changes. It's not based on your performance but anchored in His promise. You are not barely tolerated; you are deeply treasured. You are not barely hanging on; you are securely held. His love is not fragile or fickle. It's fierce, steady, and deeply personal.

So if you've ever wondered whether you've gone too far, remember—His love reaches further. If you've felt too broken, His love heals deeper. If you've felt too lost, His love finds faster. You belong to Him. Not for a season, not until you mess up again, but forever. Even on the days you question your worth or feel far from His presence, His love keeps pursuing. It never hesitates. It never runs out. You are loved. You are known. You are His—always.

Pray

Father, thank You that Your love is unbreakable and constant. Help me to live from the confidence of being Yours, not the fear of losing You. Amen.

Reflect

What one truth or moment from today's reading stood out to you?

 **LEARN**   Week 1 – Day 6

Faith in Motion Challenge

Walk it Out

Take a mindful walk or simply sit by a window and thank God for the ways He's shown His love this week. As you breathe in, remember His nearness; as you exhale, release your worries. Let gratitude steady your heart in His love.

Love in Action

Sometimes people just need a reminder that they're seen and loved. Show love this week by writing a handwritten note, leaving a sweet treat on a doorstep, or sending a text that says, "*Thinking of you today.*" Small gestures whisper God's love louder than grand speeches.

Pause & Press On   Week 1 – Day 7

Reflection & Renewal

- Which story spoke to you most this week?
- How has your understanding of God's love deepened?
- What have you begun to release into His care?
- Where do you sense new peace or renewal taking root?

Pray

Father, thank You for seeing me, pursuing me, and calling me Your own. Help me rest in Your steady love and reflect it wherever I go. Teach me to see myself as You do—chosen, cherished, and held. Amen.

Walk Together

Take a few quiet minutes to thank God for what He's revealed this week. Write a sentence or two about how His love met you in Scripture, in prayer, or in the simple moments of everyday life. Come ready to share in group, not as a polished story, but as a living testimony of His love at work in you.

Journal & Notes

Reflect on how God's love met you this week and what truth you're learning to hold.

_____

_____

_____

_____

_____

_____

_____

_____

_____

_____

_____

_____

_____

_____

_____

_____

_____

_____

_____

Journal & Notes

Reflect on how God's love met you this week and what truth you're learning to hold.

Week 2

LEAN

Loving God in Return

Week 2 – Introduction
LEAN: Loving God in Return

Love grows deeper when it's returned in trust, worship, and surrender.

Once you know how deeply you're loved, the next step is learning how to love Him back—not out of obligation, but from a grateful, genuine heart. Real love **leans** in. It listens, responds, and draws closer.

This week is about leaning into His presence through prayer, worship, and quiet trust. Loving God in return isn't about perfection; it's about posture—lifting your eyes in worship when you'd rather worry (and if you've ever tried to worship with a to-do list running in your head, you know that's its own act of faith!), choosing obedience without all the answers, and trusting His plan over your comfort.

Leaning is **devotion** in motion: staying close, listening, and loving Him not just with words, but with your life.

Sometimes it's quiet—a whispered "yes" through tears, a surrendered heart that says, *"I'll stay, even here."* As you step into this week, remember: love isn't proven by grand gestures but by steady devotion. Lean into the Love that first leaned toward you.

This week you'll explore:

- **Listening** to God and recognizing His voice
- **Worship** that flows from gratitude
- **Obedience** that deepens faith
- **Prayer** that draws you closer
- **Surrender** that brings peace

My friend, don't rush through the moments this week. The more you lean into God, the more you'll discover that He's already been leaning toward you. Each quiet prayer, each small act of trust, draws you closer to the One who's been near all along. So lean in, listen well, and let His steady love hold you there.

 **LEAN**　　　　　　　　　　　　　　　　Week 2 – Day 1

Listen with a Devoted Heart

Scripture

1 Samuel 3:10 — Speak, Lord, for your servant is listening.
John 10:27 — My sheep listen to my voice; I know them, and they follow me.

Read: 1 Samuel 3:1–10; John 10:22–30

Truth: God still speaks, and devoted hearts learn to recognize His voice.

There's something tender about learning to recognize God's voice. It's not the thunder we expect. It's the whisper that waits. Samuel discovered that as a boy in the temple. When he first heard God calling, he didn't recognize it; he thought it was Eli. But after a few gentle lessons, Samuel finally answered with one powerful phrase: *"Speak, Lord, for your servant is listening."*

That moment changed everything. Samuel didn't earn the right to hear God's voice; he just made himself available. Jesus would later describe this same kind of listening when He said, *"My sheep listen to My voice; I know them, and they follow Me."* That verse isn't about religion; it's about relationship. Sheep recognize their shepherd's voice because they've spent time near Him. The more you draw close to Jesus, the more familiar His voice becomes.

I remember a season when I kept praying for direction but felt like heaven was silent. One morning, I finally closed my journal and whispered, *"Lord, if You're speaking, help me recognize it."* I went about my day, and later a verse popped into my mind that fit my situation exactly. It wasn't a billboard moment, just a whisper. But I knew it was Him. That's when I realized: God hadn't stopped speaking; I had just been too rushed to listen.

And let's be honest, sometimes the problem isn't that God isn't speaking; it's that we're multitasking while pretending to listen. You know what I mean. We say, *"Lord, I'm listening,"* but we've got one eye on the to-do list and the other on the laundry pile that could qualify as a small mountain. If you've ever tried to pray while mentally planning dinner or checking your phone notifications, you're in good company. God doesn't roll His eyes at our distractions; He just keeps inviting us back to stillness, knowing we'll finally quiet down when we realize how much peace we've been missing.

I once joked with a friend that if God wanted to get my attention during busy weeks, He'd probably have to send a talking grocery cart. Some days, I'm halfway through the store before realizing I've been humming a worship song without even noticing. And suddenly, there He is, using aisle seven to remind me He's with me everywhere. That's the thing about His voice—it doesn't always come in church pews or prayer closets. Sometimes it slips into the middle of your everyday chaos, whispering peace where you least expect it.

Jesus said His sheep *know* His voice, and the more you spend time in His Word and presence, the easier it becomes to recognize it. He's not playing hide-and-seek with His guidance. He's building trust. Sometimes it's a whisper that brings peace where you felt fear. Sometimes it's conviction wrapped in love that redirects your path. But every time, His voice leads to life.

So if you've ever wondered why it feels hard to hear God, take heart. Even Samuel had to learn. God isn't testing your hearing; He's training your heart. Every time you pause, pray, or open His Word, you're learning the sound of your Shepherd's voice. Keep listening—it's always worth it.

And when you do hear Him—maybe through a verse, a thought, or a quiet nudge—don't rush past it. Sit with it. Let it sink in. The more you listen, the more you'll realize He's been speaking all along, right in the middle of your ordinary moments. Because that's who He is—a God who draws near, a Shepherd who knows your name, and a Father who loves to talk with His children.

If we were sitting together right now, I'd probably smile and say, *"You're hearing more than you think."* So keep leaning in, friend. His voice is closer than you realize, and it's always spoken in love.

Pray

Jesus, quiet the noise around me and the doubts within me. Teach me to recognize Your voice and trust what You say. I'm listening. Amen.

Reflect

What one truth or moment from today's reading stood out to you?

 **LEAN** Week 2 – Day 2

Worship That Overflows

Scripture

2 Samuel 6:14 — David, wearing a linen ephod, danced before the Lord with all his might.

Read: 2 Samuel 6:12-22

Truth: True love for God overflows in wholehearted worship—unashamed and authentic.

Have you ever seen someone so full of joy they just couldn't hold it in? Maybe it was a dad cheering at his kid's ball game with arms raised, shouting with pride, completely unconcerned about who was watching. That's the kind of moment we find in 2 Samuel 6. Only this time, the celebration wasn't about a game. It was about God's presence.

David had waited years for the Ark of the Covenant—the symbol of God's presence—to return to Jerusalem. When it finally arrived, he couldn't contain his joy. He danced before the Lord with all his might. No pretense. No performance. Just raw, overflowing gratitude.

Notice that David wasn't wearing his royal robes. He put on a simple linen ephod—the garment priests wore before God. The king of Israel dressed like a servant because, in that moment, he wasn't focused on status or power but on presence. His worship wasn't about image or position; it was about surrender. He wanted to be known not for his crown, but for his heart.

But not everyone got it. His wife, Michal, watched from a window and rolled her eyes. To her, it looked foolish and undignified for a king. But David didn't care. His heart belonged to God, not to public opinion. *"I will celebrate before the Lord,"* he said. Translation? My worship isn't for you. It's for Him.

I'll be honest, I didn't grow up in a church where people raised their hands. The most expressive thing we did was tap our foot or give a polite *"Amen."* The idea of lifting my hands during worship felt… well, a little too charismatic for my comfort zone. I remember the first time I even thought about it. I looked around to see if anyone was watching, then halfway raised one hand like I was volunteering for something I wasn't sure about. But in that moment, I felt something shift. Tears came, and for the first time, I understood that worship wasn't about a style or a song. It was about surrender. It was about finally realizing that I didn't have to hold anything back from the God who's never held back His love from me.

That's what happens when love for God overflows. When it moves past image, control, and fear of what others think. Worship stops being a routine and becomes a response. It's not about perfect words or polished voices. It's about a heart so aware of God's goodness that it can't help but respond.

I think about a man in my church years ago who had just finished treatment for cancer. He wasn't the expressive type—quiet, steady, the kind who blended into the back row. But one Sunday, during *Great Is Thy Faithfulness*, he lifted his hands for the first time. Tears streamed down his face. It wasn't for anyone else. It was for the One who carried him through. That, my friend, is worship that overflows.

But worship doesn't just happen in church. It shows up in kitchens, commutes, and quiet mornings. It's thanking God while folding laundry, whispering prayers in traffic, or pausing to notice His beauty in the ordinary. Worship is love made visible. An overflow of devotion that says, You are worthy, Lord, right here, right now.

And here's the beautiful part: when worship flows freely, it doesn't just honor God—it frees you. It softens pride, quiets fear, and steadies your soul. The more your eyes are on Him, the less you care about how you look doing it. So today, don't hold back. Worship like David—freely, joyfully, wholeheartedly. Whether your hands are lifted high or your heart is bowed low, let your love for Him spill over.

Pray

Lord, You are worthy of every breath and every song. Teach me to worship You with freedom and gratitude. Let my love for You overflow in joy today. Amen.

Reflect

What one truth or moment from today's reading stood out to you?

 **LEAN**　　　　　　　　　　　　　　　　　Week 2 – Day 3

Obedience That Trusts

Scripture

Genesis 22:8 — Abraham answered, "God himself will provide the lamb for the burnt offering, my son."

Read: Genesis 22:1-14

Truth Loving God means trusting Him enough to obey, even when you don't understand the "why."

Trust and obedience sound simple until God asks you to take a step that makes no sense. And if you've ever whispered, *"Lord, are You sure about this?"* — you're in good company. Abraham knew that feeling better than anyone. God had finally given him the son he'd waited decades for, the promise he'd prayed for, the one thing he loved most in the world. And then one day, God said, *"Take Isaac and offer him as a sacrifice."*

Can you imagine? Every part of that command must have felt impossible. Abraham didn't have the details. He only had the direction. Still, he got up early the next morning, gathered what he needed, and started walking. Three days of silence. Three days to turn back. Three days to wrestle with what obedience really costs.

And yet, step by step, he kept walking. Not because he understood, but because he trusted the One who had never failed him before. I imagine every step felt heavier than the last, each one a battle between fear and faith. But Abraham had learned something over the years: when God speaks, obedience always leads to blessing, even if the road to it feels unbearable.

When Isaac asked the question that must have shattered Abraham's heart, *"Father, where is the lamb?"* Abraham simply said, *"God Himself will provide."* That's the essence of faith—trusting that even when the plan doesn't make sense, the Provider never stops being who He is.

I think about seasons in my own life when God asked me to obey before I understood. Like the time I felt Him leading me to step away from something comfortable—something that made perfect sense on paper—without knowing what was next. I remember lying awake at night, staring at the ceiling, asking, "Lord, are You sure?" I even tried giving Him a few "better" ideas, but He didn't seem impressed. All I heard in return was a quiet assurance: Trust Me.

Obedience isn't easy, especially when it costs us comfort, control, or clarity. But it's in those moments that trust grows deepest. Every step of obedience says, "God, I believe You're still good, even when I can't see the outcome." And when we reach the mountain—when we finally see His provision—we realize He was never asking for what we feared to lose. He was asking for our hearts.

Abraham looked up and saw a ram caught in the thicket. God's provision waiting all along. That moment wasn't just about a test of faith; it was a revelation of God's character. He is Jehovah Jireh, the Lord who provides. And He still does.

Maybe today, God's asking you to take a step that doesn't make sense yet. To forgive when you're still hurting. To give when it feels like you don't have enough. To wait when you're desperate for movement. Friend, He sees what you can't. And His plans for you are never cruel. They are always good.

Obedience may not always feel safe, but it is sacred. Because every time you trust Him with your "yes," He proves again that He's worthy of it. And the more you say yes, the more you begin to see His fingerprints in places you once only saw uncertainty. It's in those quiet moments of surrender, when you choose to stay, go, forgive, or wait, that faith becomes more than words. It becomes a walk. You begin to realize that obedience isn't about losing control; it's about finding peace in the One who's always been in control.

Pray

Lord, help me trust You even when I don't understand. When fear or doubt whisper that obedience will cost too much, remind me that You always provide. Teach me to say "yes" quickly and completely, knowing that every step of faith draws me closer to Your heart. Amen.

Reflect

What one truth or moment from today's reading stood out to you?

 LEAN   Week 2 – Day 4

Prayer That Anchors

Scripture

Daniel 6:10 — Now when Daniel learned that the decree had been published, he went home to his upstairs room where the windows opened toward Jerusalem. Three times a day he got down on his knees and prayed, giving thanks to his God, just as he had done before.

Read: Daniel 6:10-23

Truth Loving God involves consistent communion. Prayer anchors your heart when pressure surrounds you.

There's something steadying about prayer. Not the kind that's polished or perfectly worded, but the kind that keeps showing up. The kind that whispers in the quiet, *"God, I'm still here."* That's the kind of prayer Daniel prayed. Three times a day. Not out of habit alone, but out of devotion. Prayer wasn't his backup plan when things got hard; it was his lifeline long before the storm ever came.

When the king's decree went out that no one could pray to any god but him, Daniel didn't panic, protest, or hide. He simply did what he'd always done—he went home, opened his windows toward heaven, and knelt to pray. He didn't know how it would turn out. He just knew who his God was. That's the heart of prayer—it's not about controlling the outcome but trusting the One who holds it.

That's the beauty of a life anchored in prayer. It doesn't mean trouble won't come. It means when it does, you don't crumble. Daniel didn't wait until the lions' den to find his courage. He built it in the quiet rhythm of communion with God, day after day, prayer by prayer.

I remember a time when my life felt like one long lions' den. Pressures stacked high, deadlines closing in, everything uncertain. I couldn't fix it, and honestly, I didn't even know what to pray anymore. One morning, I sat at my kitchen table with my sweet tea (yes, I know some of you coffee people are gasping right now) and simply said, *"God, I don't have the words. But You know."* That was all.

No grand prayer. Just honesty. But that moment anchored me. Because prayer isn't about the length of your words; it's about the posture of your heart.

Looking back, I can see how those quiet moments and those tear-streaked, wordless prayers were building something in me that no easy season ever could. God was teaching me that prayer isn't a task to check off; it's a tether. It holds you steady when life feels like it's pulling you apart. Even when you don't feel strong, that connection keeps you grounded in His peace and presence.

Maybe you're in a season like that right now. Maybe you're doing your best to stay faithful when the pressure is on, when the answers haven't come, when the noise around you feels louder than your prayers. Take heart, my friend. God hears the quiet prayers. The tired ones. The tearful ones. The half-sentence ones whispered between tasks. He's not impressed by eloquence. He's moved by sincerity.

Like Daniel, you can stand firm because you've knelt first. Prayer doesn't remove the lions, but it reminds you that the Lion of Judah stands with you. It gives you courage when fear roars loud and peace when the outcome is uncertain. Prayer doesn't always change your circumstances, but it always changes you. It steadies your steps, strengthens your spirit, and reminds you that you're never standing alone in the den.

So keep praying. Keep showing up. Keep opening your window toward heaven. You'll find that even when the world tries to shake you, the One who holds you is unshakable.

Pray

Father God, help me to build a rhythm of prayer that keeps me steady no matter what's happening around me. When fear or pressure rise, draw me closer instead of letting me pull away. Anchor my heart in Your presence and remind me that You are near, always listening, always faithful. Amen.

Reflect

What one truth or moment from today's reading stood out to you?

 LEAN   Week 2 – Day 5

Surrender That Strengthens

Scripture

Luke 1:38 — "I am the Lord's servant," Mary answered. "May your word to me be fulfilled."

Read: Luke 1:26-38

Truth: Loving God in return means surrendering your plans.

Surrender isn't a word we like much, is it? It sounds like giving up, like waving a white flag and losing control. But in God's hands, surrender isn't defeat. It's trust. It's saying, *"God, You can write this story better than I can."* And that's exactly what Mary did.

Mary was just barely a teenager when the angel showed up with a message that would turn her entire world upside down. *"You will conceive and give birth to a son... the Son of the Most High."* No one could have prepared her for that moment. Her mind must have swirled with questions: What will Joseph think? What will my parents say? How can this be? Yet, instead of panic or excuses, she gave one of the most powerful responses in all of Scripture: *"I am the Lord's servant. May it be to me as You will."*

That's surrender, friend. Not passive resignation, but active trust. It's choosing faith over fear, obedience over certainty. Mary didn't have all the answers. She didn't even have a plan. But she had a willing heart. And that was enough for God to move mountains through her "yes."

I remember a season when God asked me to step out of something comfortable into something completely unknown. Every part of me wanted to stay where it felt safe, where I could see what was coming next. But deep down, I knew He was calling me to something more. I argued, delayed, and prayed for a clearer sign (and maybe an instruction manual). But the peace didn't come until I finally whispered, *"Okay, Lord. I don't understand it, but I trust You."* That one surrender opened doors I never could've forced open myself. And it reminded me of another story—one that shows what faith looks like when surrender costs everything.

I once heard about a man who lost everything in a house fire. His home, his possessions, even years of work he'd poured his life into, gone in one night. Standing in the ashes, he told a reporter, "*I have nothing left but faith.*" Later, someone asked how he could still trust God after losing so much. He said, "*Because when everything burned, I saw what couldn't be taken—God's presence.*" That's surrender. Not pretending the pain doesn't hurt but choosing to trust that God's still good when everything else falls apart. It's the kind of faith that doesn't cling to outcomes, but to the One who never changes.

Maybe you've been there too. Maybe you're standing in that in-between space, caught between what you hoped for and what God is asking you to release. Surrender feels scary because it means letting go of control, but that's also where strength begins. Every "yes" to God plants a seed of courage that grows with time.

The truth is, God doesn't ask for surrender to break you. He asks for it to bless you. When you hand Him the pen, He writes a story better than the one you were clinging to.

So if your hands are trembling today, open them. Let go of what you can't control. Trust that the God who chose Mary for the impossible can handle whatever feels impossible in your own life. He's not asking you to have it all figured out—just to keep your heart willing and your hands open to Him. The same God who spoke peace to a frightened girl in Nazareth is speaking peace to you now. And when you place what you've been gripping into His hands, you'll find He's been holding you the whole time.

Surrender isn't weakness. It's worship. And when you choose it, you'll find that what feels like losing control is really gaining peace.

Pray

Lord, help me to trust You with what I can't see. Give me the courage to say "yes" even when I don't have all the answers. Teach me to rest in Your plan, knowing that Your will is always good and Your timing is always right. Amen.

Reflect

What one truth or moment from today's reading stood out to you?

 **LEAN** Week 2 – Day 6

Faith in Motion Challenge

Walk It Out

Set aside ten unhurried minutes to sit with God with no distractions, just stillness. Read a psalm or listen to a quiet worship song and ask, *"Lord, where are You inviting me to lean closer to You?"* Let your time of stillness become a song of surrender.

Love In Action

Love for God often shows up in how we serve others. Bend low for Christ this week by helping a neighbor with a small task, returning someone's grocery cart, or surprising a weary neighbor with a treat. Every quiet act of service becomes a living *"I love You"* to Him.

Pause & Press On   Week 2 – Day 7

Reflection & Renewal

- Which story or person most helped you see what loving God looks like?
- Where is it hardest for you to "lean"—listening, worship, obedience, prayer, or surrender?
- What simple practice will you make daily (time, place, plan)?
- Where did you sense new closeness with God this week?

Pray

Father, teach me to lean in close. To listen, trust, and rest in Your love. Help me love You not just in words, but in every choice and quiet act of surrender. Amen.

Walk Together

This week, as you've practiced leaning into God, take a few minutes to reflect before group. Jot down two short sentences to share: (1) where you leaned into God this week, and (2) one small next step you're taking to keep leaning closer. Come ready to share. Not polished, just honest. Sometimes your "lean" might be the encouragement someone else needs to keep walking.

Journal & Notes

Reflect on how you leaned into His presence and trusted His timing.

Journal & Notes

Reflect on how you leaned into His presence and trusted His timing.

Week 3

LET

The Heart Within Us

Week 3 – Introduction
LET: The Heart Within Us

Let God heal, renew, and refill what's been running on empty.

If Week 1 taught us how deeply we are loved and Week 2 helped us lean into that love, then this week is about letting God do what only He can do—renew us from the inside out.

We can't pour freely from an empty or wounded heart. That's why God's invitation isn't only to serve Him but to **let** Him restore us. To let means to allow, to release—to stop pretending we're fine and let His hands touch the places we've hidden. You know, those 'I'm fine, really' places we say through gritted teeth while juggling a dozen things.

Renewal starts in honesty. When we stop hiding the emptiness and hand it over, grace rushes in. Ezekiel 36:26 reminds us that God doesn't just fix the old heart—He gives us a new one, alive and beating with His Spirit. That's what this week is about: trading weary for whole, empty for full, and shame for peace.

This week you'll explore:

- A king who **let God in** and found mercy
- A woman who **let Him heal** hidden pain
- A man who **let go of his past** and found freedom
- A crowd who **let His Spirit refill** them
- Disciples who **let His peace guard** their hearts

Friend, you don't have to hold it all together. You don't have to earn the healing you need. Just let Him in. When you do, His renewal begins to move through you, and love starts to flow again—not from striving, but from overflow.

So take a deep breath, unclench your fists, and whisper, *"Lord, I'm ready. I let You in."* Then rest there. Let His presence fill every hollow space until peace begins to settle where pressure once lived. The more you let Him in, the more His love will spill out—quietly, steadily, beautifully—in every place you go.

 **LET** Week 3 – Day 1

Let God In

Scripture

Psalm 51:10 — Create in me a pure heart, O God, and renew a steadfast spirit within me.

Read: Psalm 51

Truth Renewal begins with honesty. When you invite God into the broken places, He begins to cleanse and restore.

There's a kind of exhaustion that no amount of sleep can fix. You know the kind I mean—the deep, soul-level weariness that comes from carrying things you were never meant to hold. Guilt. Regret. The constant effort of trying to hold it all together on the outside when you're falling apart inside. It's the exhaustion that makes you sigh for no reason and feel heavy even when you're sitting still.

David knew that feeling. Psalm 51 wasn't written on a mountaintop moment. It was written in the aftermath of failure. He had messed up badly, and everyone knew it. He'd hurt people, disappointed God, and broken trust. But instead of hiding behind excuses or pretending everything was fine, David did the bravest thing a person can do: he brought his mess to God. No masks. No rehearsed words. Just raw honesty. "Create in me a clean heart, O God."

You can almost feel the desperation in those words. They're not the prayer of a man trying to sound holy—they're the cry of someone who's finally done pretending. That's where renewal begins. Not in perfection, but in permission. When you stop running from the truth and start running toward the One who can handle it.

There's something sacred about letting God in like that. It's not about groveling or feeling unworthy. It's about opening up the rooms of your heart that you've kept locked. The ones cluttered with old hurts, the memories that still sting, the bitterness you thought you'd buried. Because here's the truth: what stays hidden stays unhealed. But what's revealed to God can be restored by God. To be completely open with you, there was a time when I was holding on to bitterness so tight it started shaping how I saw everything. I told myself I'd "moved on," but every time I heard that person's name, something twisted inside me. I'd smile and say I was fine, but my heart told a different story. One night, in the quiet, God nudged me gently but unmistakably, and I knew He was asking for the part I'd been protecting. I sat there and whispered, *"God, I don't want this to live here anymore."* That prayer wasn't long, but it was real. It was me letting Him in. And slowly, healing began to take root.

Maybe you know that feeling too. Maybe there's something you've been carrying—a wound, a secret, a disappointment—that you've tucked away and tried to ignore. You tell yourself you'll deal with it later, but later never seems to come. Friend, can I gently tell you something? God already knows. And He's not standing at the door with judgment; He's standing there with mercy, waiting to be let in.

The same God who met David in the rubble of regret and met me in the quiet ache of bitterness wants to meet you right where you are. Not to condemn you, but to cleanse you. To breathe peace into the parts of you that forgot what peace feels like. He's not asking you to have it all together. He's simply asking you to open the door and let Him be God again. And when you do, you'll find that His grace doesn't just meet you—it moves in, restoring what you thought was lost.

So take a deep breath. Unlock the door. Let Him in. Let His mercy fill every shadowed corner. Because when you finally stop holding it in and let God in, you won't just find forgiveness, you'll find freedom. And in that freedom, you'll rediscover joy. The kind that runs deeper than circumstance and steadier than your emotions.

Pray

Lord, I open my heart to You today. Search me, cleanse me, and renew what's grown weary or wounded. I don't want to hide anymore. Heal what's broken and fill me with Your peace. Amen.

Reflect

What one truth or moment from today's reading stood out to you?

 LET   Week 3 – Day 2

Let Him Heal What's Hidden

Scripture

Mark 5:34 — He said to her, "Daughter, your faith has healed you. Go in peace and be freed from your suffering."

Read: Mark 5:25-34

Truth Jesus heals not only what's visible, but what's been hidden for years. His touch brings wholeness and peace.

Some pain stays tucked away so long that it starts to feel like part of who you are. You learn to live around it, to function with the ache, to smile through it so no one asks questions. (And if anyone does, you've got your 'I'm fine, just tired' line rehearsed like a pro.) You tell yourself you're fine, but inside, you know you're not. The woman in Mark 5 knew that kind of pain. Twelve years of bleeding. Twelve years of doctors, disappointments, and isolation. She had spent everything she had trying to get better, yet instead of healing, she only grew worse.

I imagine she stopped expecting things to change. The shame, the loneliness, the whispers when she walked by—it all must have become normal. But then she heard about Jesus. Something in her stirred, a flicker of hope she hadn't felt in years. She didn't need attention or a stage—just one touch of the edge of His robe.

That's the thing about hidden pain. It rarely makes a scene, but it runs deep. And sometimes, like her, we reach for healing quietly, hoping maybe this time it'll be different. She didn't ask permission or announce her need. She just reached out in faith, and Jesus stopped everything. He turned, looked right at her, and called her daughter. Not outcast. Not problem. *Daughter.* One word of belonging after twelve years of feeling invisible.

Healing begins there—in that moment of recognition. When Jesus sees not just what's wrong with you, but the person underneath the pain. His touch didn't just stop her bleeding; it restored her identity. She came trembling, but she left in peace.

I think about a story I once heard of a woman who carried invisible wounds from her childhood. Years of words that told her she wasn't enough. She grew into a woman who looked strong, successful, respected, but inside she was still that little girl trying to earn love. One night, sitting alone after another long day of striving, she whispered, *"God, I don't want to live like this anymore."* She said she felt a peace wash over her. For the first time, she didn't feel like she had to prove her worth. She realized she was already loved deeply, completely by the God who made her.

That's what Jesus does. He doesn't just heal what others can see; He restores what's been hidden and hurting for far too long. You don't have to clean it up or make sense of it before you come to Him. You just have to reach out, even if it's trembling.

Friend, maybe you've been living with something unseen. A quiet grief, a wound that never healed right, a secret shame that still whispers lies. Whatever it is, Jesus isn't afraid of it. He doesn't flinch from your pain; He moves toward it. His healing might not always look instant, but His presence is immediate. He meets you in the mess and begins mending what you thought was too broken to fix.

So come close. You don't have to shout or prove or earn. Just reach out. Let Him meet you where the pain still lingers. Because one touch from His grace can do what years of trying never could. It can make you whole again. And when He does, you'll realize healing was never about becoming who you were—it's about becoming who you were always meant to be.

Pray

Jesus, You see the parts of me no one else does—the hurts I hide, the fears I bury, the wounds I've learned to live with. Thank You for loving me there, for calling me "beloved" when I feel broken. Today, I reach for You. Heal what's hidden, restore what's weary, and remind me that Your touch still brings peace that lasts. Amen.

Reflect

What one truth or moment from today's reading stood out to you?

_____

 LET   Week 3 – Day 3

Let Go of the Past

Scripture

Philippians 3:13-14 — Forgetting what is behind and straining toward what is ahead, I press on toward the goal to win the prize for which God has called me heavenward in Christ Jesus.

Read: Genesis 41:50-52 and Philippians 3:7-14

Truth Healing happens when you release the hurt.

Some things are easier to forgive than to forget. You might move on in words, but deep down, part of you still lives in the memory replaying what was said, what was lost, what should've been different. You tell yourself you're over it, but a song, a name, or a smell pulls it all back like it happened yesterday. That's the tricky part about the past. It doesn't stay put when pain has roots.

Joseph understood that. He'd been betrayed by his brothers, thrown into a pit, sold as a slave, and imprisoned for a crime he didn't commit. He had every right to stay bitter. Every reason to rehearse the injustice. But when God finally lifted him up and gave him a family of his own, Joseph named his first son Manasseh, which means, "God has made me forget all my trouble." That didn't mean he had amnesia—it meant he chose release. He decided not to let old wounds write his next chapter.

That's what letting go really looks like—it's not pretending it didn't happen; it's choosing not to carry it anymore. Because the longer you hold onto hurt, the heavier it becomes. (It's like dragging around an overstuffed suitcase you swore you'd unpack years ago.) Healing starts when you stop rehearsing what broke you and start remembering who can restore you.

Paul said it this way in Philippians 3: *"Forgetting what is behind and straining toward what is ahead, I press on"*—because that's more than a mindset; it's a movement. Letting go isn't passive; it's active faith. It's choosing to loosen your grip on what's behind so you can reach for what God has waiting ahead. You can't run freely while holding onto yesterday. God invites you to trade your backward glance for forward motion.

You ever think you've moved past something, only to realize it's still renting space in your heart? I've been there. I was carrying something I didn't even realize was weighing me down. Someone had said something offhand, but it stuck. For years, I let those words define me. Every time I tried to step into something new, that old voice whispered, "You're not enough." Then one day, I felt the Lord nudge my heart: "You're holding onto words I never said." That stopped me cold. I realized I'd built a wall to protect myself, but it was keeping me from growing. Letting go didn't happen overnight, but that was the start—laying those words at His feet and walking away empty-handed, but free.

My friend (we'll call her Beth) once told me about the anger she'd carried toward her dad for years. He'd left when she was little, and even though she grew up and built a life of her own, that hurt followed her everywhere. One day, while praying, she sensed God whisper, *"You don't have to keep punishing him to feel safe anymore."* That moment undid her. Tears came, but so did freedom. She realized letting go wasn't about pretending it didn't matter—it was about releasing the power it had over her heart.

Friend, maybe there's something in your past that still echoes. A betrayal, a disappointment, a wound that shaped the way you see yourself. You can't change what happened, but you can choose what happens next. You can stay stuck in what hurt you, or you can hand it over to the One who can redeem it.

Letting go isn't weakness. It's worship. It's saying, *"God, I trust You more than my need to make sense of this."* It's opening your hands so He can fill them with something new—peace, purpose, and the freedom to love again without fear.

So today, remember Joseph. Remember Paul. Remember the woman who forgave. And most of all, remember the Savior who let go of heaven's glory to hold you instead. The past might have shaped you, but grace defines you.

Pray

Jesus, You know the things I still cling to and the memories I can't let go. I place them in Your hands. Heal what's broken and help me trust You. Amen.

Reflect

What one truth or moment from today's reading stood out to you?

 LET   Week 3 – Day 4

Let His Spirit Refill You

Scripture

1 Kings 19:4–5 — While he himself went a day's journey into the desert. He came to a broom tree, sat down under it and prayed that he might die. "I have had enough Lord," he said. "Take my life; I am no better than my ancestors." Then he lay down under the tree and fell asleep!

Read: 1 Kings 19:1–18

Truth When you're weary and worn, God doesn't push you harder — He refills you with His presence, peace, and power.

There's a kind of tired that no nap can fix. You know the kind—the exhaustion that settles in your soul. The kind that makes you want to pull the covers over your head and say, "Lord, I've had enough."

Elijah knew that kind of weariness. One day he was calling down fire from heaven; the next, he was running for his life, terrified and spent. He ended up in the wilderness, under a broom tree, whispering words that sound a lot like burnout: *"I've had enough, Lord."*

It's comforting to me that this mighty prophet—the one who saw God's power firsthand—still hit a breaking point. Because it means that faith doesn't make us superhuman. It makes us dependent.

What I love most about this story is how God responded. He didn't lecture Elijah for his lack of faith or tell him to get it together. He sent an angel with a meal and let him sleep. Twice. No shame. No scolding. Just grace. (If it were today, maybe the angel would've shown up with a warm blanket and a casserole.) Because sometimes the most spiritual thing you can do is rest, eat, and let God remind you that you're not alone.

After Elijah rested, God met him again. Not in the wind, or the earthquake, or the fire, but in a gentle whisper. That quiet voice refilled what fear had drained. The same God who showed His power on Mount Carmel now showed His tenderness in the wilderness. He gave Elijah food for his body, a whisper for his spirit, and direction for his next step.

I've had broom tree moments too—those days when I sit at my kitchen table, sweet tea in hand, staring at the same to-do list and thinking, *Lord, I don't have another ounce to give.* And every time, God meets me there—not with lightning or guilt, but with a gentle reminder: *"You don't have to carry this alone."*

Maybe that's where you are today. You've been strong for everyone else. You've kept showing up, kept serving, kept smiling—but inside, you're running on fumes. Friend, God isn't asking you to push through. He's asking you to pause. To sit under your own broom tree for a bit and let Him refill you.

Let Him feed you with His Word. Let Him refresh you with His Spirit. Let Him remind you that even when you feel done, He's not done with you. Elijah thought his story was over, but God had more work for him, and more grace to give him.

So, if your soul feels tired today, take heart. The same God who sent food to Elijah sends rest to you. The same whisper that steadied the prophet still speaks to your weary heart. Lean into it. Let it quiet the noise and restore your strength.

Because when you let His Spirit refill you, you don't just get back up. You rise renewed, ready, and reminded that you were never walking alone. His strength begins where your striving ends, and what once felt like the end of your rope becomes the beginning of His restoration.

Pray

Lord, I'm tired. Not just in body, but deep down in my spirit. Meet me under my broom tree today. Quiet the noise, refresh my soul, and refill me with Your peace and power. Help me to rest in You until my strength returns. Amen.

Reflect

What one truth or moment from today's reading stood out to you?

_____

_____

 LET   Week 3 – Day 5

Let Peace Guard Your Heart

Scripture

Philippians 4:6-7 — Do not be anxious about anything, but in everything, by prayer and petition, with thanksgiving, present your requests to God. And the peace of God, which transcends all understanding, will guard your hearts and your minds in Christ Jesus.

Read: Mark 4:35-41

Truth God replaces anxiety with peace when you release control and rest in His presence.

If there's one thing I've learned, it's that peace doesn't usually show up when everything is calm. It shows up when everything isn't. The kind of peace Paul talks about isn't found in the absence of storms but in the presence of Jesus right in the middle of them.

Honestly, I'm not the best at letting go of control. I like plans, lists, and knowing what's next. But peace doesn't live in my planner. It's not penciled in between errands and emails. It comes from surrender. There was a season when I kept praying for calm circumstances, but what God kept offering instead was calm within me. One night, I laid in bed replaying every 'what if'— what if this doesn't work out, what if that goes wrong. I finally sighed and whispered, *"Lord, I'm tired of being my own security system."* And I felt Him say, *"Then let Me guard your heart."*

It reminded me of that story in Mark 4, when the disciples panicked in the storm. The waves were crashing, the boat was rocking, and Jesus… was asleep. I love that detail. He wasn't ignoring them; He was illustrating peace. The kind of peace that's so rooted in trust it doesn't flinch when life starts tossing things around. When they woke Him, He didn't scold them for being scared. He simply spoke to the storm, and the sea obeyed. The peace that calmed the waters that night is the same peace He offers you and me.

Sometimes, though, it's not a raging sea that steals our peace. It's a slow drip of worry that seeps in little by little. It's that text you're waiting on, the medical result that hasn't come, the child you can't quite reach, or the future that feels too uncertain. Anxiety doesn't always roar; sometimes it just hums in the background until your spirit feels frayed. That's why Paul said to bring everything to God in prayer—because even the "small stuff" matters to Him.

I'll never forget one particularly stressful week when I tried to juggle too much at once—deadlines, family things, church commitments, and a mountain of laundry that might've qualified as a national park. I was snapping at everyone and feeling guilty about it, when I finally stopped, took a deep breath, and said out loud, *"Okay, Lord, I quit trying to be in charge."* It sounds silly, but I could almost feel the tension leave my shoulders. The situation didn't magically fix itself, but my heart quieted down. That's what happens when we hand it over—peace doesn't just arrive; it guards.

Friend, maybe you're in a storm today and you've been trying to row your way out. Know this, Jesus is still in your boat. You don't have to control the waves; you just have to stay close to the One who can calm them. When you pray and release it to Him, you're not giving up. You're letting peace take its rightful place as the guard over your heart.

So tonight, before you fall asleep, try this: instead of running through your list of worries, thank God for one thing He handled today. One thing you didn't have to fix. Let gratitude anchor you. Let His presence steady you. Let His peace keep watch, and let the weight you've been carrying rest where it belongs—in His hands. Even if tomorrow feels uncertain, He's still faithful, and He's still right there with you.

Pray

Jesus, I confess that sometimes I hold on and try to control what only You can calm. Teach me to release my worries and rest in Your peace. When storms rise or anxiety creeps in, remind me that You are with me, and You are enough. Guard my heart and mind today, and let Your peace be what guides my steps. Amen.

Reflect

What one truth or moment from today's reading stood out to you?

 LET   Week 3 – Day 6

Faith in Motion Challenge

Walk It Out

Clean out a small space like your desk, a drawer, or a closet. As you sort, pray: *"Lord, help me release what no longer belongs."* Let the act of decluttering become a picture of what He's doing inside your heart—making space for peace and renewal.

Love In Action

When someone's worn thin, even small kindnesses can feel like healing. Think of someone who's weary and offer to run an errand, drop off a care basket on their porch, or bring them their favorite drink as a small surprise. Gentle compassion has a way of carrying God's touch straight to the heart.

Pause & Press On   Week 3 – Day 7

Reflection & Renewal

- What part of your heart has God been healing this week?
- Is there a past hurt or fear you've begun to release?
- How can you make space for God's Spirit to refill you daily?
- Where do you sense new peace or renewal taking root?

Pray

Faithful Messiah, I let You in. Heal what's weary, fill what's empty, and make my heart new again. Meet me in the quiet places and remind me that Your presence is enough. Help me rest in Your renewal and live from the overflow of Your love. Amen.

Walk Together

As you wrap up this week, pause and thank God for the ways He's been working in your life—restoring what's weary, refreshing what's dry, and reminding you of His steady love. Write down what stood out most in your time with Him, and come ready to share how His presence has met you this week.

Journal & Notes

Reflect on what you let go of and how God's renewal is taking root.

Journal & Notes

Reflect on what you let go of and how God's renewal is taking root.

Week 4

LIVE

Walking in Faith

Week 4 – Introduction
LIVE: Walking in Faith

Let faith be your footing. You don't have to see it all to start walking.

Before we can **live** out our faith, we have to understand what walking by faith really means—not the kind that depends on perfect conditions, but the kind that keeps moving when the path is uncertain. The kind that trusts God even when life feels foggy and His hand seems hidden.

This week is about real, everyday faith—the kind that shows up in small steps, quiet prayers, and stubborn hope. It's not flashy or flawless. Sometimes it's moving forward; sometimes it's standing still when your heart wants to sprint ahead.

Faith doesn't require a map; it just requires **trust**. God rarely gives us the whole plan, but He always gives us Himself. Every act of **obedience** becomes a quiet declaration: *"I don't have to know the way to follow the One who does."*

So, friend, as you step into this week, remember: you don't need perfect confidence, just willing steps. The same God who called you to walk will keep you steady with every step you take.

This week you'll explore:

- Stepping **when you can't see**
- **Fixing our eyes on Jesus** instead of the storm
- **Walking faithfully** through the waiting
- **Standing with courage** when fear whispers loud
- **Finding strength** in God when yours runs out

You don't have to know the whole plan to take the next step. So tie your shoes, lift your chin, and whisper, *"Lord, I trust You."* Then start walking, because faith grows in motion—and it grows stronger each time you choose to keep walking.

And if you trip along the way? Don't worry, you're in good company. Every great step of faith in Scripture started with one small, sometimes shaky yes. God's not looking for perfection; He's looking for movement. One step at a time is enough when your eyes are on Him.

 LIVE Week 4 – Day 1

Step Forward in Faith

Scripture

Genesis 12:1 — The Lord had said to Abram, "Leave your country, your people and your father's household and go to the land I will show you."

Read: Genesis 12:1-9

Truth Faith begins with obedience. Sometimes God doesn't show the whole map—just the next step.

Have you ever wished God would just hand you a detailed itinerary for your life? You know—dates, directions, maybe a color-coded chart so you'd know exactly when to turn left or right? I've prayed that prayer more than once: *"Lord, I'll gladly follow You, just send me the spreadsheet."* But faith doesn't work that way (it's less like Google Maps and more like "trust fall"). God doesn't hand out diagrams. He gives invitations.

That's what happened to Abram. One ordinary day, God told him, *"Leave everything familiar, and I'll show you where we're going."* No address. No timeline. Just a promise. If it had been me, I probably would've said, *"Show me the land first, then I'll start packing."* But Abram didn't negotiate; he obeyed. He took the first step, not because he had all the details, but because he trusted the One giving the directions.

Faith starts small. One step. One "yes." One moment of obedience when everything in you wants to wait for a little more information. Sometimes that step looks like forgiving someone you're not ready to forgive. Sometimes it's starting the thing you've been too afraid to try. Other times, it's simply choosing peace when worry feels easier.

I'll never forget when God nudged me to start something new that made absolutely no sense. I had more questions than answers, and I might've argued (just a little). *"Lord, are You sure You've got the right person?"* But deep down, I knew what He was asking: *"Trust Me."* So I did—hesitantly, imperfectly, one small step at a time. And wouldn't you know it? Every time I took a step, He met me there. Not before, not all at once, but right when I needed it.

That's how faith works. It grows as you go. God rarely shows us the finish line first because He wants to walk with us through the middle. If He gave you the whole plan upfront, you might run ahead—or run away! But when He gives it piece by piece, it keeps you close enough to hear His voice saying, *"This way."*

I once heard a story about a man who decided to follow his GPS instead of his gut. It told him to take a "shortcut" through a back road that turned out to be a muddy cow pasture. He kept going anyway slowly, cautiously until his tires sank and there he was, stuck in the middle of nowhere while the GPS cheerfully repeated, *"Continue straight for three miles."* (He didn't make it.) Later, he laughed and said, *"I trusted the wrong voice."* It's funny, but it's also a little convicting, isn't it? We do that too. We follow the loudest voice instead of the right one. Faith isn't about perfect directions; it's about following the One who never leads you into a ditch.

And let's be honest, if life came with turn-by-turn directions, we'd probably still get lost. (Some of us can't even follow GPS without a *"rerouting"* warning.) The good news? God's grace reroutes too. When you take a wrong turn, He doesn't revoke the promise; He redirects the path.

We all have those crossroads where comfort feels safer than calling. But God's direction often starts with disruption. Not because He wants to confuse us, but because He wants to draw us closer. So, friend, whatever "next step" God's been whispering to your heart, take it. You don't have to see the whole journey to start moving. The same God who called Abram out of the familiar is calling you forward too. You can trust Him with the unknown because He's already there, waiting for you.

Pray

Jesus, thank You for calling me to walk by faith, not by sight. When I want the whole plan, remind me that Your presence is my map. Give me courage to take the next step, even when I can't see what's ahead. I trust You to lead, provide, and meet me on the path. Amen.

Reflect

What one truth or moment from today's reading stood out to you?

 LIVE　　　　　　　　　　　　　　　　Week 4 – Day 2

Step Out of the Boat

Scripture

Matthew 14:29 — "Come," He said. Then Peter got down out of the boat, walked on the water and came toward Jesus.

Read: Matthew 14:22-33

Truth Faith grows when you trust Jesus more than the waves. Fear fades when your eyes stay on Him.

Have you ever prayed for God to move, and then panicked a little when He actually did? I think Peter would understand.

The disciples were out on the water when a storm kicked up, waves tossing the boat like a toy. Then, in the middle of the chaos, they saw someone walking toward them on the water. Naturally, they freaked out. (Because, honestly, if I saw someone strolling across a lake at 3 a.m., I'd need more than prayer—I'd need a life jacket and possibly therapy.)

But it wasn't a ghost—it was Jesus. And He said something simple, yet life-changing: *"Take courage! It is I. Don't be afraid."*

Peter, ever the bold one, called out, *"Lord, if it's You, tell me to come to You on the water."* And Jesus did. So Peter climbed out of the boat, one trembling foot after another, and for a moment, he did the impossible.

But then he looked around. The wind howled. The waves rose. Fear whispered louder than faith, and he began to sink. *"Lord, save me!"* he cried. And immediately—don't miss that—*immediately* Jesus reached out and caught him.

That's the part I love most. Jesus didn't wait to see if Peter could swim back on his own. He didn't scold or shame him for doubting. He just reached. That's who He is—quick to save, steady to hold, faithful to lift us when our faith falters. And maybe that's what faith really looks like—not walking perfectly, but reaching back when He reaches for us.

Sometimes, we give Peter a hard time for sinking, but honestly? He's the only one who even got out of the boat. The others stayed where it felt safe, clinging to what they could control. But not Peter. He stepped out. And even though he stumbled, he experienced something the rest never did—the feeling of standing on faith, right there with Jesus.

I think we've all had "boat moments." Times when we felt God nudging us to do something outside our comfort zone—to start the ministry, have the hard conversation, take the job, forgive the person, or trust again after being hurt. And just like Peter, we start strong… until we notice the wind. Fear whispers that we're not qualified, not ready, not enough. That's when our faith wobbles, and we start sinking back into safety.

I remember once agreeing to speak at an event even though the thought of public speaking made me want to run for the hills. I prayed, I prepared, and I nearly backed out (three times) before the day came. But as I stood there—knees knocking, heart racing—I whispered, *"Lord, I'm stepping out. You'll have to carry me."* And He did. My voice shook, my notes fluttered, but His presence was steady. I didn't walk on water that day, but I sure learned how to trust the One who could calm the waves.

Here's the truth: Jesus doesn't call you out to embarrass you; He calls you out to grow you. He's not waiting for you to sink. He's inviting you to see what's possible when your eyes stay on Him.

So, friend, if He's calling you to take a step of faith, don't let fear stop you. The waves may rise, the wind may roar, but your Savior's already standing in the middle of it, hand extended, ready to catch you if you fall. You were never meant to live anchored in fear. And if your steps are wobbly, remember, Jesus doesn't grade balance; He honors bravery. You were made to walk in faith.

Pray

Jesus, thank You for calling me to trust You even when I'm afraid. When I start to sink in doubt or fear, remind me that You're near and ready to catch me. Amen.

Reflect

What one truth or moment from today's reading stood out to you?

 LIVE   Week 4 – Day 3

Step Through the Waiting

Scripture

Joshua 6:15-16 — On the seventh day, they got up at daybreak and marched around the city seven times in the same manner... When the priests sounded the trumpet blast, Joshua commanded the people, "Shout! For the Lord has given you the city!"

Read: Joshua 6:1-20

Truth Faith means walking even when it feels repetitive or delayed. God's promises are worth the persistence.

Have you ever felt like you were walking in circles, waiting on God to move? You keep praying, keep showing up, and yet... nothing seems to change. You wonder, "Am I getting anywhere, or am I just doing laps around the same problem?"

That's where we find Joshua and the Israelites. God promised them victory over Jericho, but the plan probably didn't make much sense: march around the walls once a day for six days, then seven times on the seventh day. No ladders, no weapons, no shortcuts. Just walking and waiting. Imagine how strange that must've felt. Day after day, circling the same walls, hearing the same silence, and seeing no visible progress.

If I'd been there, I'd have been the one asking, "*Joshua, are we sure we're not lost? Maybe we missed a turn.*" Someone probably asked for directions, and Joshua just kept walking. But that's the thing about faith—it often looks repetitive long before it looks rewarding.

Sometimes God's greatest victories come after the longest seasons of obedience. The Israelites' marching didn't make the walls fall—their faith did. Every step was a declaration: We still believe. Every lap was an act of trust: We still obey. And on the seventh day, when they shouted, God moved.

Waiting seasons can feel like walking in circles too. You pray for healing, but the diagnosis doesn't change. You ask for breakthrough, but the door stays shut. You keep giving your best, but nothing seems to shift. It's easy to wonder if your obedience is doing anything at all. But here's what Jericho teaches us: just because you don't see progress doesn't mean God isn't working behind the walls.

If I'm honest, there was a time I prayed for something for what felt like forever. I had faith, at least at first, but after months of silence, I started praying a little less passionately. You know, those *"Lord, do what You're gonna do"* kind of prayers. (Not exactly the faith-filled shout of Jericho.) But one morning, months later, I woke up to an unexpected message. A door I'd given up on suddenly swung wide open. God hadn't forgotten; He'd just been preparing everything behind the scenes while I was circling in trust. That line stuck with me through my own waiting seasons.

I once heard someone say, *"The seventh lap only matters if you didn't quit after the sixth."* That's what faith looks like—showing up on lap six with the same obedience you had on lap one, even when the walls haven't budged yet.

And sometimes, while we're waiting for the walls to fall, God's doing His best work in us. He's strengthening endurance, stretching trust, and deepening character. The waiting isn't wasted; it's worship in motion.

So, friend, if you're in a Jericho season right now, keep walking. Keep praying. Keep believing. You may not see the cracks forming, but they're there. The God who brought down walls with a shout can handle what's standing in your way. One more lap might be all it takes. So keep walking, because faith doesn't sit still. It circles, it prays, it persists, and it presses on.

Pray

Jesus, thank You for being faithful even when I can't see the progress. When I grow weary in the waiting, remind me that You're working behind the walls. Give me strength to keep walking, persistence to keep trusting, and faith to keep circling until Your promise comes through. Amen.

Reflect

What one truth or moment from today's reading stood out to you?

___

 LIVE   Week 4 – Day 4

Step with Courage

Scripture

Esther 4:14 — And who knows but that you have come to your royal position for such a time as this?

Read: Esther 4:10-16

Truth Walking in faith sometimes means standing in courage. God uses our obedience to bring deliverance.

There are moments in life when faith looks less like walking and more like standing your ground, with your heart pounding, knees shaking, whispering, *"Lord, please help me do this, even if I'm afraid."* That's where we find Esther. She wasn't a warrior, a preacher, or a prophet—just an ordinary young woman placed in an extraordinary position. And isn't that how God often works? Using ordinary hearts to fulfill divine purposes.

That's where we find Esther. She wasn't a warrior, a preacher, or a prophet. She was an ordinary young woman placed in an extraordinary position. And isn't that how God often works? Ordinary hearts in divine moments. When her people were in danger, her cousin Mordecai sent her a message that changed everything: *"Who knows but that you have come to your royal position for such a time as this?"*

But there was one problem—approaching the king without being summoned could mean death. Imagine the fear pulsing through her veins. She could stay silent and safe or speak up and risk everything. Her decision wasn't easy, but her faith was real. *"I will go to the king,"* she said, *"and if I perish, I perish."*

That's courage—not the absence of fear, but obedience in spite of it. Esther didn't know the outcome; she just knew the One who called her to act. And when she stepped forward in faith, God used her bravery to save an entire nation.

I think we all face "Esther moments." Times when God calls us to stand up, speak truth, or take action when it would be easier to stay quiet. Maybe it's sharing your faith when you'd rather blend in. Maybe it's confronting injustice, extending forgiveness, or doing the right thing when it costs you comfort. Faith doesn't always look like crossing oceans—it often looks like opening your mouth, even when your voice trembles.

I once watched a friend show that kind of courage in a way that changed me. She'd been wronged publicly and had every reason to defend herself. Instead, she prayed first, waited, and responded with grace instead of anger. It wasn't flashy or dramatic—just quiet strength. And watching her, I realized courage doesn't always roar. Sometimes it whispers, *"I'll trust God to fight this one for me."*

And let's be honest, courage doesn't usually feel courageous in the moment. It feels messy and uncertain. It's like standing on the edge of the diving board, heart racing, trying to talk yourself into jumping. You know you'll survive the jump, but your stomach still flips. The same is true with faith. You might feel scared, but you jump anyway because you trust the One waiting in the water.

Here's the truth: God doesn't ask you to be fearless. He asks you to be faithful. When you take a brave step, He fills the gap between your trembling and His triumph. Courage isn't something you have before the moment; it's something that shows up when you need it most.

So, friend, whatever "such a time as this" moment you're standing in, take heart. You don't have to have it all together. You just have to step forward. God has already gone before you, and He's already working through your obedience. You never know who might find freedom because you chose to be brave. Courage in motion is faith in motion—one trembling step that God turns into a testimony.

Pray

Jesus, thank You for being my courage when I feel afraid. When I'm tempted to shrink back, remind me that You go before me and stand beside me. Give me faith to obey even when it costs something and trust that my small steps of courage can make a lasting difference. Amen.

Reflect

What one truth or moment from today's reading stood out to you?

 LIVE Week 4 – Day 5

Step Into God's Strength

Scripture

2 Corinthians 12:9 — *But he said to me, "My grace is sufficient for you, for my power is made perfect in weakness." Therefore, I will boast all the more gladly about my weaknesses, so that Christ's power may rest on me.*

Read: 2 Corinthians 12:7-10

Truth Real faith depends on God's strength, not our own. Weakness is where His power shines brightest.

We live in a world that celebrates strength. Strong opinions, strong resumes, strong coffee. (I'll skip the coffee part, thank you very much.) But the truth is, sometimes faith doesn't look strong at all. Sometimes it looks like showing up tired, whispering prayers through tears, and saying, *"Lord, I can't do this without You."*

Paul knew that feeling. He had what he called a *"thorn in the flesh"*—something painful that wouldn't go away no matter how many times he asked God to remove it. Three times he pleaded, and three times God said no. But not because He didn't care. Instead, God said, *"My grace is sufficient for you, for My power is made perfect in weakness."*

In other words, Paul, I'm not taking the thorn away—I'm going to use it.

That's hard to hear when you're in the middle of your own thorn season, isn't it? We like the idea of victory, not vulnerability. We want mountain-top strength, not valley lessons. But Paul discovered something life-changing: when you stop trying to prove how strong you are, God finally gets the room to show how strong He is.

There was a stretch when I was running hard on empty. Meetings, deadlines, and commitments stacked higher than the laundry. I thought if I could just push through, it would all settle down. Instead, I ended up on my living-room floor surrounded by half-finished to-dos, whispering through tears, *"Lord, I'm done."* And in that moment, I felt Him whisper back, *"Good. Now let Me carry it."*

It made me laugh through the tears because it's true—I can be stubborn. (I know I'm not alone here!) We like to say, *"God helps those who help themselves,"* but that's not biblically defensible. The truth is, God helps those who surrender themselves.

I once heard someone compare life to a three-legged race with God. You're tied to Him and He's right beside you, but when you try to run ahead or drag behind, you trip. The only way to move smoothly is to match His pace, step for step. That's what strength in faith looks like. Not sprinting on your own, but staying in sync with Him.

When we let God's strength fill our weakness, something shifts. The weight feels lighter because we're no longer carrying it alone. The fear feels smaller because we know who's holding us up. And the pressure to perform fades because His grace is enough.

So, friend, if you're feeling weary or worn thin today, take heart. You don't have to have it all together for God to use you. In fact, that's where His power shines brightest—in the cracks, in the tears, in the *"I can't, but He can."* Let Him be your strength today.

Because maybe the point isn't to be unshakable—it's to know where to lean when life shakes you. God isn't asking you to hold it all together; He's asking you to hold onto Him. When your knees feel weak, His arms are steady. When your courage runs out, His grace keeps flowing. So rest easy, dear one. You're not failing—you're learning what faith really looks like: leaning hard on a God who never lets go.

Pray

Jesus, thank You for being strong when I am weak. When I reach the end of myself, remind me that's where Your strength begins. Teach me to lean on Your grace, and let Your power shine through my weakness. Amen.

Reflect

What one truth or moment from today's reading stood out to you?

_____

 LIVE   Week 4 – Day 6

Faith in Motion Challenge

Walk It Out

Go for a drive or walk and talk with God about what's ahead. Whether it's a winding road or a snowy sidewalk, let the journey remind you that faith isn't about seeing the whole path. It's about trusting Who's walking with you. Let it become an act of surrender and courage.

Love In Action

Faith grows stronger when it walks beside someone else's. Think of someone who's waiting, hurting, or walking through uncertainty, and drop off a meal, offer a listening ear over coffee, or send them something that lifts their spirit. Remind them they're not walking alone.

Pause & Press On   Week 4 – Day 7

Reflection & Renewal

- Where has God asked you to take a step of faith recently?
- How did obedience strengthen your trust?
- What fear or "waves" try to pull your focus off Jesus?
- What truth from this week will help you walk boldly into next week?

Pray

Lord, I trust You with the steps I can't see. Steady my heart when fear whispers and remind me that faith grows with every step I take toward You. Keep me walking in Your strength, one step at a time. Amen.

Walk Together

As you close this week, take a moment to look back on every step of faith you've taken—big or small. Reflect on how God met you in the waiting, how He strengthened your courage, and how His promises have held true. Write down one story, verse, or moment from this week that encouraged you most, and bring it to share in our group session. Your story might be the very reminder someone else needs to keep walking by faith.

Journal & Notes

Reflect on what steps of faith stretched you and how He kept you steady.

Journal & Notes

Reflect on what steps of faith stretched you and how He kept you steady.

Week 5

LIFT

Loving Others in Action

Week 5 – Introduction
LIFT: Loving Others in Action

Faith isn't meant to stay put—it's meant to move.

If the first few weeks were about loving God and letting Him reshape your heart, this week is where that love gets legs. It's time to **lift!** To take what's been growing inside and put it into motion.

Don't worry, you don't have to start a ministry or move overseas (unless God says so—then call me first so I can pray and maybe pack snacks).

Love in action shows up in the small, sacred things: a kind text, a dropped-off meal, grace for a sharp tone, or a smile for the grumpy cashier. Compassion is love in motion. It notices, serves, and stays even when it's inconvenient.

This week is all about seeing people the way Jesus did—serving with humility and carrying others through prayer and practical love. Because love isn't a feeling we keep inside; it's a faith we live out.

When we lift others, we reflect the heart of Jesus—serving with **compassion**, grace, and humility. Love in action doesn't wait to be noticed; it simply shows up.

But remember, friend, we can lift because He lifted us first—from sin to salvation, from shame to grace. Every act of love is simply our way of carrying forward the strength He's already given us.

This week you'll explore:

- **Seeing the need** through God's eyes
- **Serving with humility** and joy
- **Loving "the least of these"** with dignity
- **Carrying others** to Jesus in prayer and action
- **Bearing one another's burdens** with compassion

So grab your sweet tea (and maybe a notepad for all the ways God will nudge your heart this week), and let's lift together. Because when love rises, hearts heal, and faith moves farther than we ever imagined.

 **LIFT** Week 5 – Day 1

Seeing the Need

Scripture

Luke 10:33 — But a Samaritan, as he traveled, came where the man was; and when he saw him, he took pity on him.

Read: Luke 10:25-37

Truth Compassion begins with seeing. God calls us to notice those in need and respond, not look away.

There's a big difference between *seeing* and *noticing*. Seeing is passive. We move through our days, glancing at faces, scrolling past posts, registering problems and people without a second thought. Noticing, though, is active. It means pausing, paying attention, and letting compassion shape our response.

That's what happened in Jesus' parable of the Good Samaritan. A man was beaten, robbed, and left for dead. Two religious men saw him but passed by on the other side. They didn't stop being believers that day. They just didn't let belief interrupt their schedule. Then came a Samaritan, the least-expected hero. He didn't walk by, scroll past, or make excuses. He saw the man—really saw him. And that one moment of compassion changed everything.

I wish I could say I always stop, but truthfully, I've had plenty of "cross-to-the-other-side" moments. The times I spot the need, feel the nudge, and still think, *"Maybe later."* Once I drove past a neighbor I knew was struggling and told myself I'd check in later. When I finally did, she said, *"I was hoping someone would come by."* Talk about conviction. God reminded me that compassion starts with noticing. Not when it's convenient, but when it's needed.

Here's the sweet surprise: sometimes the biggest blessing isn't for the person you help. It's for you. When you "cross the road," something shifts inside. Compassion softens what busyness hardens. It breaks through the noise and reminds you that your purpose isn't found in checking off lists, but in loving people well. Every act of mercy rewires your perspective. God will often remind you of that truth in the simplest places. You start to see people, not problems.

You find joy you didn't expect, peace you didn't know was missing, and connection that makes your faith feel alive.

And sometimes, friend, noticing is as simple as looking up from your own chaos. I once stood in line at the grocery store, half-distracted and wondering if my cart (mostly frozen dinners and sweet tea) qualified as a cry for help. The cashier looked exhausted, so I smiled and asked how her day was. She blinked like no one had asked all week and said, *"You just made it better."* It cost nothing but attention, and God reminded me that compassion doesn't always wear a cape. Sometimes it just wears a smile.

Another time, I thought I was being helpful by "seeing the need" for my husband to mow the lawn sooner. I pointed it out (twice). He didn't find my compassion nearly as inspiring as I did. (Apparently, noticing isn't the same as nagging. Who knew?) We laughed about it later, but it hit me: true compassion doesn't criticize. It comes alongside. It lifts, not lectures.

Here's the thing, when you ask God to open your eyes, He will. He'll show you the coworker whose brave face is slipping, the teen who needs encouragement, the neighbor who's lonely. It can feel uncomfortable, inconvenient, or even awkward. But compassion was never meant to fit neatly on a to-do list. It's meant to stretch your heart and interrupt your schedule a little, because that's often where love does its best work.

Compassion doesn't wait for the perfect moment. It begins with open eyes and a willing heart. When we start noticing the hurting, the lonely, or the overlooked, God begins to work through us in ways we never imagined. So today, ask God to slow your steps and open your eyes. Look for the one on the side of the road. That coworker who's been quieter than usual. The friend who used to show up but doesn't anymore. The stranger who looks like they've had a long day. Compassion is love in motion, and it starts with seeing.

Pray

Jesus, open my eyes to the needs around me. Slow me down enough to notice, and give me the courage to respond. Help me see others the way You do. Amen.

Reflect

What one truth or moment from today's reading stood out to you?

 LIFT	Week 5 – Day 2

Serving with Humility

Scripture

John 13:5 — After that, He poured water into a basin and began to wash His disciples' feet, drying them with the towel that was wrapped around Him.

Read: John 13:1-17

Truth True love stoops low. Serving others in humility reflects the heart of Christ more than grand gestures.

When we think of serving, we often picture something big like mission trips, meal trains, or organizing an entire event. But Jesus showed us that true service starts smaller. Can you imagine this scene? The Savior of the world, the One who spoke galaxies into being, got down on the floor to wash dirty feet.

If anyone ever had the right to skip the humble jobs, it was Jesus. Yet there He was, kneeling with a towel and basin, serving the very people who would soon betray, deny, and abandon Him. That moment wasn't about footwashing. It was about heart posture. Jesus didn't serve to earn something; He served because He already was something—secure, loved, and obedient to His Father.

That's what humble service looks like: doing what needs to be done, not for recognition, but from love—*agape* love. The kind that gives without keeping score, serves without seeking attention, and shows up even when it's inconvenient. It's folding the towels no one notices, listening when you'd rather talk, or saying *"I'll do it"* when everyone else suddenly finds something else to do. Agape love doesn't ask, What's in it for me? It simply says, *"If this helps someone else, I'm in."*

Honestly, humility and I have had a few tug-of-war moments. I once volunteered to help at a church event thinking I'd be greeting people or leading a table discussion. Turns out, I got assigned to bathroom duty. As I stood there with toilet paper roll in one hand and Lysol in the other, I muttered something about *"serving the Lord with gladness,"* though my tone wasn't exactly joyful. Somewhere between the mop and the paper towels, God whispered, *"This counts too."* And you know what? It did. That quiet, unseen service softened something in me that pride never could.

Picture this: you've finally sat down after a long day, feet up, dinner done, and someone calls from the other room, *"Hey, can you help me for a sec?"* You sigh, because you *just* got comfortable. But you get up anyway. Five minutes later, whatever needed doing is done—the trash is out, the sink's unclogged, the lightbulb's changed—and somehow, your attitude's lighter too. That small act of service didn't just help someone else; it lifted you. That's the quiet reward of humility. It refocuses your heart faster than any sermon ever could.

The truth is, when we serve with humility, something shifts inside us. It changes the way we see people… and ourselves. Serving doesn't make you less; it makes you more like Jesus. It takes your eyes off your own importance and opens your heart to the beauty of obedience.

And humility isn't weakness. It's strength under control. The kind that chooses gentleness when pride wants to prove a point. It's the quiet courage to serve without needing credit, trusting that God sees what others overlook. It's the power to say, *"I'll go low so someone else can rise."* When we serve without spotlight or applause, heaven leans in and says, *"That looks like Me."* And in those hidden moments, our hearts learn what real greatness feels like.

So whether it's washing dishes, mentoring a teen, or helping someone who can never repay you, remember, love doesn't need a platform. It just needs a towel.

Don't underestimate the small stuff. The greatest ministry often happens in the ordinary, where no one's watching but God. Every humble act whispers worship, reminding the world, and your own heart, that Jesus is still in the business of serving through willing hands.

Pray

Jesus, teach me to serve like You with humility, joy, and love that doesn't seek attention. Help me see every act of service, big or small, as worship. Amen.

Reflect

What one truth or moment from today's reading stood out to you?

 LIFT   Week 5 – Day 3

Serving the Least of These

Scripture

Matthew 25:40 — The King will reply, "I tell you the truth, whatever you did for one of the least of these brothers of mine, you did for me."

Read: Matthew 25:31-40

Truth This is the Truth passage of Faith in Motion. It moves people because Jesus identifies Himself with the hungry, thirsty, and forgotten. Focus on the surprise—*"When did we see You?"*—to show that love often happens unnoticed.

It's one thing to say we love Jesus; it's another to love like Him. What surprises us in Matthew 25 is how closely He ties the two together. He doesn't say, *"When you preached a great sermon"* or *"When you impressed the crowd."* He says, *"When you fed, clothed, visited, or cared—you did it for Me."*

That means every small act of compassion is personal to God. The meal you deliver, the listening ear you offer, the time you take to check on someone—it all reaches His heart. Jesus doesn't distance Himself from the suffering; He identifies with it. The hungry, the lonely, the overlooked. They aren't just people we help. They're reflections of Him.

And that question from the people, *"When did we see You?"* always gets me. They weren't trying to earn gold stars for kindness. They were simply living out love, one unnoticed act at a time. Their compassion wasn't planned, posted, or perfect—it was genuine. They didn't even realize their service had eternal weight. Isn't that just like God? To take our ordinary moments and turn them into something sacred.

I remember one summer afternoon when I was grilling a few hot dogs for lunch and felt a quiet nudge to take one over to my neighbor. I didn't know her well, and part of me thought that she'd think I'm strange showing up with a hot dog on a paper plate. But the prompting wouldn't go away, so I went. She opened the door, surprised, and when I handed her the plate, she just stared for a moment before tears filled her eyes. Later she told me she'd been sitting alone that afternoon, ready to give up. She had a bottle of pills nearby and was thinking of ending her life. That one small, awkward act of obedience interrupted her despair long enough for hope to breathe again. It still humbles me to think how God used something as simple as a hot dog to remind someone that she was seen, loved, and worth saving. That day changed the way I saw serving—it's rarely about grand gestures; it's about quiet obedience.

Imagine this: You're rushing through your day, juggling work, errands, and maybe a kid's science project that involves way too much glitter. You pause to help someone who's struggling. Maybe you carry their groceries, send a quick message of encouragement, or stop long enough to listen. It feels small, almost forgettable. But heaven takes note. Because Jesus says, *"That was Me you just served."* Suddenly, what looked ordinary becomes holy ground.

Sometimes we hesitate to serve because we think what we have to offer isn't enough. We forget that love doesn't measure in size; it measures in sincerity. God isn't looking for perfect service, just willing hearts. He can take our small and make it sacred.

The beauty of this passage is its simplicity. Love that looks ordinary to the world looks extraordinary to Jesus. A cup of water. A visit. A kind word. A shared hot dog. Every time we meet a need, we meet Him there too. And every time we meet a need, we serve our Faithful Messiah who met all of ours.

So today, keep your eyes open for Jesus in disguise. He may not look like what you expect, but He's there—waiting in the faces of those who just need to be seen, fed, encouraged, or loved. And when you love them, even in the smallest ways, you'll discover that Jesus was standing on both sides of the exchange all along. Because every time love moves, so does heaven.

Pray

Jesus, open my eyes to see You in the faces of those I encounter today. Teach me to love without hesitation and to serve without seeking recognition. Remind me that when I care for others, I'm really caring for You. Amen.

Reflect

What one truth or moment from today's reading stood out to you?

 LIFT　　　　　　　　　　　　　　　　　　　Week 5 – Day 4

Carrying Others to Jesus

Scripture

Luke 5:19 — When they could not find a way to do this because of the crowd, they went up on the roof and lowered him on his mat through the tiles into the middle of the crowd, right in front of Jesus.

Read: Luke 5:17-26

Truth Love lifts. When we carry others through faith, prayer, and presence, God does what we cannot.

Some stories in Scripture just stay with you, and this one always does for me. Four friends carrying a paralyzed man to Jesus. Not because it was easy, but because it was worth it. When the crowd blocked their way, they didn't turn around or make excuses. They climbed a roof, tore it open, and lowered their friend right down in front of the Healer. That's what true love in action looks like—determined, creative, and unwilling to give up.

I always picture the moment Jesus looked up and saw not just the man on the mat, but the faces of his friends peeking through that hole in the ceiling. Scripture says, *"When Jesus saw **their** faith*, He said, 'Friend, your sins are forgiven.'" That line gets me every time. It wasn't just the man's faith that moved Jesus; it was the faith of those who refused to stop believing on his behalf.

Maybe that's what we're all called to do—to be roof-climbers for someone else's faith. To carry the weary when they can't carry themselves, to lift them when they've run out of strength, and to place them right where healing can happen. Sometimes that looks like prayer. Sometimes it's showing up with a meal, a ride, or a listening ear. Sometimes it's just sitting quietly and holding space when words fall short.

I often think about those four friends and whisper a quiet prayer: *"Lord, when I'm the one who's down and can't move, I hope I have friends who will carry my mat and lower me to You."* Because truthfully, we all take turns being the one on the mat and the one doing the carrying. Some seasons we're strong and full of faith. Other times, we're just hanging on, needing someone else's faith to steady us. Both are holy places. And that's why it's so important to make sure we have those kinds of friends—the ones who will carry our mat when we can't carry ourselves. The ones who don't walk away when the road gets hard, but walk us right to Jesus instead.

And let's be honest, sometimes carrying the mat isn't graceful. We trip over our own feet, bump into walls, or drop the corner we were supposed to be holding. Loving people can get messy. But Jesus never asked for perfect balance, just willing hearts. Even when we stumble, He steadies the load and makes sure no one gets left behind. Because love in motion doesn't quit—it just finds another way. Heaven celebrates the effort, not the elegance.

Picture this for a moment: Someone you know is struggling. Maybe not physically, but emotionally or spiritually. They can't find their way back to hope. You can't fix it, but you can carry them in prayer, lift them through encouragement, or help lighten their load. That's what it means to love like Jesus—to show up when it's hard, to keep believing when they can't, and to trust that He can do what we can't.

And don't miss this part of the story: the man walked out that day healed, but so did the hearts of his friends. When you help carry someone to Jesus, He strengthens you too. Your faith grows deeper, your love stretches wider, and your compassion starts looking more like His.

So maybe today, ask God who's lying on a "mat" in your world—someone who needs to be carried in prayer, lifted in encouragement, or simply reminded they're not alone. Because when love lifts, heaven moves. And maybe, just maybe, the same love that helps them rise will lift something in you too. That's how God works—healing both the carried and the carrier.

Pray

Jesus, thank You for friends who carry me when I can't stand. Open my eyes to those who need lifting today, and give me faith that won't quit. When I'm weak, send others to carry my mat, and let my love always lead others to You. Amen.

Reflect

What one truth or moment from today's reading stood out to you?

 **LIFT**　　　　　　　　　　　　　　　　　Week 5 – Day 5

Bearing One Another's Burdens

Scripture

Acts 2:44-45 — All the believers were together and had everything in common. Selling their possessions and goods, they gave to anyone as he had need.

Read: Act 2:42-47

Truth Love lives in community. We lift others when we share, pray, and walk together in faith.

If you've ever tried to carry something heavy by yourself like a couch, a box of books, or maybe just a week that's been a lot, you know how much easier it gets when someone grabs the other end. That's what the early church understood so well. Acts 2 paints a picture of people doing life together. They prayed, shared meals, met needs, and showed the world what love looks like when it moves in both directions.

They didn't form a committee or vote on who was most deserving. They just noticed, cared, and gave. Their love wasn't theoretical; it was tangible. Someone needed food, and someone else brought it. Someone was struggling, and another came alongside. That's what it means to bear one another's burdens—to lift together so no one falls apart alone.

Could you imagine what that would look like in today's world? Neighbors pulling up with casseroles and lawnmowers instead of competing Amazon deliveries. People texting, *"I'm heading to the store. Need milk or just moral support?"* Imagine Facebook filled with prayer chains instead of complaint threads! Can you picture a world where believers are tripping over each other to give instead of to be seen? It'd be holy chaos, but the best kind!

I remember one season when life felt heavy for me. There were bills to pay, projects to finish, and a whole pile of *"I'll get to it later"* stacked higher than the laundry. Out of nowhere, a friend showed up at my door with dinner and said, *"You looked tired on Facebook."* (Apparently, exhaustion has a filter.) We sat, ate, laughed, and prayed. By the time she left, my burden hadn't disappeared, but it definitely felt lighter. God has a way of using people to remind us we're not supposed to do this walk of faith solo. I'll never forget that night. That moment opened my eyes to how God works through the quiet, ordinary gestures of others.

That moment opened my eyes to how God works through the quiet, ordinary gestures of others. That's what real community is—not perfect people with color-coded planners and spotless kitchens, but a family of believers learning to show up for each other. Sometimes that looks like a meal or a prayer. Other times, it's just sending a text that says, *"Hey, you're on my heart today."* Small things, done in love, add up to something big in the Kingdom.

Let's be honest though, bearing burdens can be messy. Sometimes we don't know what to say, or we're afraid of making things worse, so we pull back. But love shows up anyway. You might trip over your words or show up with store-bought cookies instead of homemade, but that's okay. God isn't grading the presentation. He's looking at the posture of your heart. He just wants us to walk beside each other and keep showing up.

The beauty of the early church wasn't in their perfection but in their presence. This was just weeks after the resurrection. Jesus had ascended, the Holy Spirit had come, and these brand-new believers were learning how to live out their faith together. They didn't have programs or polished sermons; they simply had each other. That's where joy multiplied, faith deepened, and needs were met. When one rejoiced, they all celebrated. When one suffered, they all prayed. That's what love looks like when it breathes in unity.

So today, ask God to show you someone who's carrying something too heavy alone. Offer to help shoulder it with a prayer, a meal, or even a listening ear. And if you're the one under the weight, let someone in. Because sometimes the bravest thing you can do is let another believer lift your end of the couch.

Pray

Jesus, thank You for the gift of community. Help me notice when others are struggling and step in with grace. Teach me to share the load. Amen.

Reflect

What one truth or moment from today's reading stood out to you?

 LIFT   Week 5 – Day 6

Faith in Motion Challenge

Walk It Out

Take a "prayer tour" of your contact list or social media feed. As you scroll, ask God to show you who needs encouragement or prayer. Let this simple act of intercession lift others and remind you that your prayers truly move His heart.

Love In Action

Love lightens the load when life feels heavy. Lift someone's spirit this week by helping carry groceries, picking up a prescription, or dropping off a few essentials for someone who's struggling. Kindness in motion is often the clearest reflection of God's compassion.

Pause & Press On   Week 5 – Day 7

Reflection & Renewal

- Who did God place in your path this week that you hadn't noticed before?
- How did you experience His love flowing through you, not just to you?
- What surprised you about serving or forgiving others?
- How did these actions affect your own heart and faith?

Pray

Father God, thank You for showing me how to love like You. Help me keep my eyes open to the needs around me. Teach me to serve with humility, to forgive with grace, and to lift others as You have lifted me. May my faith express love. Amen.

Walk Together

As you close this week, take time to look back at all God has revealed. Reflect on how love lifted you and how He used you to lift others. Write down one story or moment that stood out—a time when compassion turned into action or when someone carried you. Be ready to share it in our group session as a testimony of what happens when faith moves from intention to impact.

Journal & Notes

Reflect on where you lifted others in love and how God lifted you.

Journal & Notes

Reflect on where you lifted others in love and how God lifted you.

Week 6

LIGHT

Living on Mission

Week 6 – Introduction
LIGHT: Living on Mission

Live lit by love. With Jesus close, the ordinary turns holy.

If you've ever tried to light your way with a dying flashlight, you know how frustrating it is. The beam flickers, the batteries fade, and before long you're bumping into things wondering what went wrong. The good news? Jesus never runs low. He's the Light of the World—steady, bright, and unchanging—and we get to carry that light wherever we go.

This week is all about learning how to live lit (the holy kind, not the trendy kind). We'll talk about reflecting Christ's **light**, leading others toward Him, and shining even when life feels dark. Because sometimes, it's the everyday obedience—the small yeses and quiet faithfulness—that guide someone else home.

The early believers didn't keep the light to themselves. They carried it into every corner of the world. That same **purpose** still burns in us today. When we stay connected to the Source, His light moves through us—spilling into workplaces, homes, and neighborhoods in ways only He can orchestrate.

Remember, friend, light was never meant to stand still. It moves, it spreads, and it leads the way for others to see Him more clearly. Keep walking, keep shining, and trust that every small act of love keeps His light in motion.

This week, we'll explore:

- The **light of Christ** that shines through you
- The ordinary moments God uses to **lead others home**
- The **power of praise** that breaks through the darkness
- The joy of **multiplying God's mission** wherever you go
- The **steady faith** that finishes strong

By the end of this week, I pray you feel recharged and reminded that your life matters on mission. You don't have to preach a sermon or move across the world to make a difference—just stay plugged into Jesus and shine right where you are. So grab your coffee (or mason jar of tea), settle in, and let's talk about what it means to carry the light—not just in words, but in motion.

 LIGHT Week 6 – Day 1

Reflecting the Light of Christ

Scripture

John 8:12 — When Jesus spoke again to the people, he said, "I am the light of the world. Whoever follows me will never walk in darkness, but will have the light of life."

Read: John 8:12; Matthew 5:14-16; 2 Corinthians 4:6

Truth: We don't create the light. We reflect it. Jesus is the Source, and our lives become mirrors of His love and truth.

If you've ever tried to take a selfie in bad lighting, you know how important the right light is. No filter, no angle, and no amount of "hold still, I think this one's better" can fix a picture taken in the dark. I've learned this the hard way. Every time I try, the glare from my glasses gives me two glowing green circles for eyes. (Apparently, that's not the heavenly glow I was going for.) Spiritually, it's the same. We can't create our own light; we can only reflect the One who already shines perfectly.

When Jesus said, *"I am the light of the world,"* He wasn't handing out flashlights; He was offering Himself. Following Him means walking in His glow, not trying to generate our own. That takes the pressure off, doesn't it? The light that shines from us is really His love bouncing off a surrendered heart.

And here's the thing about reflection, it depends on proximity. The closer we are to the Light, the clearer our reflection becomes. Move too far away, and that brightness fades fast. Not because the Light changed, but because we did. Spending time with Him in prayer, in His Word, and in stillness will make you start glowing in places you didn't even realize were dark.

I once noticed this in the most unexpected way. My car was parked under a streetlight one night, and it was so dirty that it looked dull gray instead of silver. But when the light hit it just right, it still shimmered, grime and all. That's us with Jesus. We don't have to be spotless to reflect His light; we just have to stay close enough for it to hit us. He's not looking for perfection, just connection.

Peter learned that the hard way. After denying Jesus three times, he must have felt like his light had completely gone out. But when the risen Christ met him on the shore in John 21 and asked, *"Do you love Me?"* three times, He wasn't shaming Peter. He was restoring him! One moment in the presence of Jesus rekindled what shame had dimmed. The same man who once hid in the shadows later preached so boldly that thousands came to faith. That's what happens when the Light gets hold of a surrendered heart—it shines through every crack.

And maybe that's the point: we don't have to produce light to be useful to God; we just have to pass it along. A kind word, a listening ear, a small act of love. They all carry a bit of His glow into someone else's darkness. Every reflection matters. You may never know who's finding their way because your life quietly lit the path.

So if you're feeling a little spiritually dim today, don't panic. You don't need to burn brighter; you just need to turn closer. His light never fades, never flickers, and never depends on your performance. Stay near the Source, and you'll shine naturally. Let His presence soak into the corners of your soul until His glow becomes your calm, His warmth your courage, and His reflection your joy. Even on the dim days, His light still holds you.

Because when the world looks dark, the solution isn't for us to shout louder. It's for us to shine clearer. Light doesn't argue with darkness. It just shows up and wins. So keep showing up. Keep reflecting. Keep letting His love spill through the cracks of your humanity until the people around you can't help but see a little more of Him. And when they do, may they realize what we've come to know, that the Light isn't just something we carry, it's Someone who carries us.

Pray

Jesus, thank You for being the Light of the World, and the light in my world. Draw me close so that Your love, grace, and truth shine through me. When others see my life, let them see You shining back. Amen.

Reflect

What one truth or moment from today's reading stood out to you?

 LIGHT　　　　　　　　　　　　　　　　Week 6 – Day 2

Leading Others Home

Scripture

Acts 8:29 — The Spirit told Philip, "Go to that chariot and stay near it."

Read: Acts 8:26-40

Truth: God uses ordinary moments to lead others toward Him. When we're sensitive to His prompting, our obedience shines light on someone's path.

Have you ever felt that little nudge from God? The one that whispers, *"Go talk to them,"* or *"Send that text,"* and you immediately thought, *"Surely, Lord, You meant someone else/"* Same here! Philip probably could've said that too when an angel told him to leave a thriving ministry and head down a desert road. No map, no itinerary, no explanation—just *go*. And he did. That's how one faithful step led him to a man who was searching for truth and didn't even know it yet.

I love how ordinary the setup is. There's no crowd, no microphone, no church service—just one traveler in a chariot and another walking nearby. Philip didn't deliver a sermon; he started a conversation. Sometimes that's all it take. He simply asked, *"Do you understand what you're reading?"* and listened. That question opened the door for the *euangelion*, the Greek word for the good news of Jesus. And that man went home rejoicing. Sometimes the most powerful ministry looks less like a spotlight and more like a quiet, obedient "yes."

I once had a moment like that, though mine involved a store parking lot instead of a chariot. I saw a woman crying in her car and felt a tug in my heart to go check on her. My first thought was, *"Lord, that's weird. She'll think I'm selling something."* But I couldn't shake it, so I walked over and asked if she was okay. She told me her mom had just passed away, and she didn't want to go home alone. We stood there crying together, holding hands by the shopping carts. I didn't have the right words, but somehow Jesus showed up between the tears and the traffic.

Sometimes God's nudges feel small or a little awkward, but they're always on purpose. He's not looking for eloquence; He's looking for obedience. You might stumble over your words, question your timing, or feel like you have nothing to offer. But the Spirit isn't looking for perfect delivery. He just needs a willing heart. And the funny thing is, when we show up for others, we often realize He was showing up for us too.

That's the beauty of being led by the Spirit. We don't have to have a plan, just a posture of availability. God does the heavy lifting; we just show up and hold the flashlight. You never know when your "go stand by that chariot" moment might come. It could be a text, a note, or a small act of kindness that reminds someone they're seen and deeply loved by God. Sometimes the Spirit whispers in the middle of a gas station run or during the world's slowest red light, and before you know it, you're part of a divine appointment you never scheduled. Trust me, obedience rarely comes with details. It just comes with direction.

And friend, if you ever wonder whether your obedience matters, remember this: the Ethiopian went home carrying the gospel to an entire region because one man listened and obeyed. One moment of faithfulness can ripple farther than you'll ever see. Philip didn't stay to watch the impact; he simply followed the next nudge, trusting that God would finish what He started. That's the quiet miracle of obedience—it echoes in hearts and places we may never touch this side of heaven.

So today, slow down and listen for the gentle promptings of the Spirit. They might sound small, but heaven is often hidden in the simple. You don't need to chase a platform; just follow His path. You may never know how far your obedience travels—but God does. And when we move in step with Him, even the smallest "yes" becomes a beam of light in someone's darkness, guiding hearts quietly home. What a joy to think that our everyday moments could help lead someone home.

Pray

Jesus, thank You for trusting me with divine interruptions. Help me recognize Your voice and respond with a willing heart. Use my ordinary moments to point someone toward You. May my steps, words, and presence shine with Your light and help lead others home. Amen.

Reflect

What one truth or moment from today's reading stood out to you?

 LIGHT   Week 6 – Day 3

Shining Through the Darkness

Scripture

Acts 16:25 — About midnight Paul and Silas were praying and singing hymns to God, and the other prisoners were listening to them.

Read: Acts 16:16-34

Truth: Light shines brightest in darkness. Even in hard seasons, praise and perseverance point others to Christ.

You can learn a lot about someone by how they handle midnight. Not the *"I drank too much sweet tea and can't sleep"* kind of midnight, or the *"one more episode"* kind. But the heavy kind—the one that hits your heart when life feels unfair or uncertain. Paul and Silas found themselves in that kind of darkness. Beaten, chained, and thrown into jail for doing good. If anyone had the right to grumble, it was them. But instead of complaining, they sang. And not the quiet kind of singing, either. Scripture says the other prisoners were listening.

Can you imagine that moment? The smell of damp stone, the sound of chains, the ache of bruises—and through it all, the sound of two men worshiping. Oh, how their voices must have echoed beautifully against the cold walls, the notes bouncing off stone and iron until the whole prison became a cathedral of praise. What a beautiful thing, that a place meant for punishment became a place of presence. Sometimes our own "prisons," the hard seasons we never asked for, become the perfect places for beauty to rise. Don't you just love how God has a way of turning echo chambers of pain into sanctuaries of grace?

A friend once told me about a time she lost her job unexpectedly. It was one of those gut-punch moments where the rug feels pulled from under you. She said she sat in her car crying, feeling angry and afraid. Until a worship song came on the radio. For some reason, she started singing along through the tears. She said, *"I didn't even believe the words yet, but I sang them anyway."* That moment became a turning point. It didn't fix everything, but peace started seeping in. Praise doesn't erase pain, but it often invites God right into the middle of it. That's faith in motion—singing truth while your heart's still catching up.

And she's in good company. Think about King Jehoshaphat in 2 Chronicles 20. When an army came against him, he didn't call for more weapons. He called for the worship team. They led with praise before the battle was even won. And as they sang, the Lord fought for them. It's almost as if heaven leans in closer when we worship through the worry. Whether it's a battlefield, a prison cell, or a parking lot, God's power meets us right where our praise begins.

I've never been in a prison like Paul and Silas, but I've had my share of midnight moments. Seasons where I couldn't see the next step and didn't feel much like singing. Maybe you've been there too. When life closes in and joy feels hard to find, praise can feel like the last thing you want to do. But sometimes praise is the only thing that keeps the darkness from winning.

Sometimes the hardest songs are the ones you sing in the dark. One night, when everything felt heavy, I sat in my bedroom after work, exhausted and teary-eyed. I didn't have a song in me, so I just whispered, "*Jesus.*" That was it. No melody, no words. Just His name. And in that stillness, I felt His peace settle over me. It didn't change my circumstances, but it changed me. Sometimes that's what worship does. It turns the key of your heart even when the doors around you haven't opened yet.

The next time you find yourself in a hard place, remember Paul and Silas. The world may be watching how you handle the midnight. You don't have to sing perfectly or loudly, just faithfully. Because your praise, even whispered through tears, still echoes. And that kind of light never goes unnoticed.

When we praise through the pain, we declare that our hope isn't chained to our situation—it's anchored in our Savior. The same God who shook the prison doors for Paul and Silas is still shaking chains today, one song, one prayer, one act of faith at a time.

Pray

Jesus, when darkness feels close, remind me You're closer. Help me praise and trust You're working even now. Let my faith shine, even in the dark. Amen.

Reflect

What one truth or moment from today's reading stood out to you?

 LIGHT   Week 6 – Day 4

Multiplying the Mission

Scripture

Matthew 28:19-20 — Therefore go and make disciples of all nations, baptizing them in the name of the Father and of the Son and of the Holy Spirit, and teaching them to obey everything I have commanded you.

Read: Matthew 28:18-20

Truth: God's mission becomes ours. When we go, serve, and share, His light multiplies through every act of faith.

When Jesus spoke these words, He wasn't giving the disciples a travel itinerary. He was giving them a purpose. "Go" wasn't about packing bags or booking flights; it was about stepping into the world with hearts on mission. The same Spirit that sent them out still whispers to us today: Shine where I've placed you.

Jesus gave this command not to perfect preachers or polished leaders, but to regular folks—fishermen, tax collectors, doubters, and friends who still smelled like the sea. They'd stumbled, scattered, and questioned, yet Jesus still chose them to carry His message forward. Isn't that just like God? To hand eternity's greatest assignment to imperfect people with hearts willing to say "yes."

And here's the beautiful thing, the mission of God has never been a solo act. It's a relay. Jesus handed the torch to His followers, who handed it to others, who eventually handed it to us. We're part of a long, unbroken line of light carriers stretching from the dusty roads of Galilee to your neighborhood street. And somehow, God thought to include us. Every time we love, serve, forgive, or speak truth, we're passing that flame forward.

Sometimes "going" looks like crossing oceans, but more often it looks like crossing the street. It's checking on a neighbor, mentoring a student, or praying with a coworker. It's choosing to live in such a way that others catch a glimpse of Jesus before you ever say His name. The world doesn't need louder Christians; it needs brighter ones.

I remember hearing about a man who carried his Bible to work every day. Not to make a statement. He just read it on his lunch break. For months, no one said a word. Then one day, a coworker sat down and asked quietly, *"Can I read with you?"* He never preached a word, but his quiet consistency spoke volumes. That simple act—no sermon, no spotlight—became the doorway to faith. The mission multiplied, one lunch break at a time.

And isn't that just how God works? His kingdom grows through ordinary people doing small, faithful things. You never know whose faith might be sparked because you chose to show up, speak up, or simply live differently. The light doesn't stay contained; it spreads. It's contagious—in the best possible way.

And that's the beauty of the gospel in motion: it multiplies in the ordinary. Every prayer whispered for a hurting friend, every meal shared with someone who feels forgotten, every act of forgiveness that breaks the cycle of bitterness. These are seeds of the Kingdom. You don't have to change the whole world; just change the world for one person. And before you know it, the light you carried becomes the light they pass on too.

So today, remember you carry the flame of the Great Commission. You don't have to have all the answers, just a willing heart and a "yes" on your lips. The same Jesus who sent the disciples promises to go with you too. And when you shine, others find their way home. Every act of love becomes a spark in someone else's darkness. Every word of grace fans the flame a little brighter.

Friend, keep saying yes. Keep carrying the light. Your glow might be the first glimpse of hope someone's seen in a long time. The world is watching for the light that leads them to our Faithful Messiah.

Pray

Jesus, thank You for trusting me with Your mission. Help me see each moment as a chance to share Your light. Give me courage to go where You lead, love who You place before me, and reflect You in all I do. Amen.

Reflect

What one truth or moment from today's reading stood out to you?

_____

 LIGHT   Week 6 – Day 5

Finishing Faithfully

Scripture

2 Timothy 4: 7 — *I have fought the good fight, I have finished the race, I have kept the faith.*

Read: 2 Timothy 4:6-8

Truth: Faith in motion doesn't fade — it endures. Living on mission means staying faithful until the finish, keeping our eyes on the eternal reward.

Some people start strong but fade fast. Others stumble early but finish with a fire that never goes out. Paul was one of those finishers. After years of preaching, traveling, and enduring more hardship than most of us could imagine, he could finally say, *"I've finished the race."*

And he didn't say it from a place of comfort or success. He said it from a prison cell, waiting for his final breath. That's the kind of faith that doesn't quit when life gets hard. It keeps going because it knows the finish line leads to Jesus.

I think about all the "races" we run in life—work deadlines, family responsibilities, dreams we chase, and detours we never planned for. Some days we sprint; other days we crawl. But faithfulness isn't measured by speed—it's measured by persistence. God isn't standing at the finish line tapping His foot; He's running beside us, matching our pace, cheering us on with every step.

Let's be honest, some days this "race of faith" feels less like a graceful run and more like a three-legged race where you're tied to your own clumsy self. There are detours, shoe blowouts, and moments when you swear you're running uphill both ways. But the beauty is, God doesn't hand out trophies for style points. He delights in the ones who just keep moving, even if it's with a limp, a laugh, and a whole lot of grace.

And if you've ever felt like quitting, you're not alone. I've had seasons where my faith felt more like a shuffle than a stride. Where I was just trying to make it to the next day without tripping over my own doubt. But those are often the moments when endurance is being built. Sometimes faith looks like fiery passion, and sometimes it looks like quiet persistence choosing to believe even when you don't feel it.

Paul's words remind us that finishing faithfully doesn't mean finishing flawlessly. It means running with purpose, even when the path is rough. It means trusting that every act of obedience, every prayer whispered in secret, and every tear shed along the way is seen by the One who rewards in eternity. The crown he talks about isn't made of gold. It's the joy of hearing Jesus say, "*Well done, good and faithful servant.*"

I once watched a marathon where one runner fell just a few feet before the finish line. Instead of staying down, she crawled—bruised, exhausted, determined—until she crossed. The crowd went wild, not because she was the fastest, but because she finished. That's what faith looks like. It's messy and gritty and glorious all at once. We may limp across the line, but we'll cross it in His strength, not ours.

Watching her made me think about our own race of faith—how every stumble and scrape just makes the finish line that much sweeter. And when that finish line finally comes into view, I like to think Jesus will be there waiting—not just with a crown, but maybe with a glass of the sweetest tea we've ever tasted. (Because let's be honest, we've earned a good porch sit after this race!) Heaven's refreshment never runs out, and neither does His joy.

So if your steps feel slow today, don't lose heart. You're still in the race. Keep your eyes fixed on Jesus—the Author, the Sustainer, and the Finisher of your faith. The goal isn't to outpace anyone else; it's to finish faithfully, hand in hand with the One who never left your side. And when you cross that finish line, He'll be waiting with arms open wide and joy overflowing. Every step, every tear, every act of faith becomes part of the radiant story that led you home—a story lit by His grace and glowing with His glory.

Pray

Jesus, thank You for staying beside me. When I'm weary, remind me You've already won. Give me strength to finish faithfully and love that lasts to the end. Amen.

Reflect

What one truth or moment from today's reading stood out to you?

 **LIGHT** Week 6 – Day 6

Faith in Motion Challenge

Walk It Out

Step outside at dusk or dawn, or simply gaze through the window, and notice how even the faintest light changes the darkness. As you watch, whisper: *"Lord, make my life a reflection of Your light."* Let that quiet moment rekindle your mission to shine wherever you go.

Love In Action

Light spreads through warmth, not perfection. Shine His love this week by bringing joy to someone's day—flowers for a neighbor, baked goods for a fire station, or a thank-you card for your mail carrier. Every bit of light you share helps someone else see Him more clearly.

Pause & Press On   Week 6 – Day 7

Reflection & Renewal

- Where has God placed you to shine right now?
- What fears or excuses have dimmed your light?
- How has your understanding of purpose changed through this study?
- What next step will you take to keep your faith in motion?

Pray

Father, thank You for calling me to shine Your light. Help me reflect Your love in every season and remind me that Your presence still shines through me. Let my life glow with grace and compassion that points others to You. Amen.

Walk Together

As you close this week and this journey, take a moment to pause and remember all that God has revealed. Reflect on how His light has met you in unexpected places. Come ready to share what He's taught you and how you've seen His light move, both in you and through you.

Journal & Notes

Reflect on how His light has shined through you and where He's calling you to keep shining.

Journal & Notes

Reflect on how His light has shined through you and where He's calling you to keep shining.

Conclusion
The Journey Continues

Faith in Motion: Walking Out What You've Learned

If you've made it this far, take a deep breath (and maybe a sip of sweet tea) because you've just walked through six beautiful, stretching, sacred weeks. You've learned about God's relentless love for you, leaned into loving Him in return, let Him heal and refill your heart, lived out steps of faith, lifted others with compassion, and finally, shined your light into the world. That's no small thing, friend. That's transformation in motion.

Each week was a step. Not toward perfection, but toward presence. Toward a deeper walk with the God who sees you, knows you, and chooses you. And as you've moved through these pages, His love has been moving through you—changing how you see Him, yourself, and the people around you.

Because Faith in Motion has always been about more than a study—it's a way of life. It's about waking up every day and choosing to walk love out, even when it's messy, inconvenient, or unseen. It's about hearing God's whispers in the ordinary, finding peace in the pauses, and joy in the serving. It's about letting your heart become a living reflection of His.

If there's one thing I pray you carry from this journey, it's this: **You are deeply loved, completely known, and purposefully sent.** God didn't fill your heart just to make it full. He filled it so it could overflow. The world around you is waiting for the kind of love only He can pour through you.

So keep walking, friend. Keep loving. Keep lifting. Keep shining. Let your faith stay in motion—one conversation, one act of kindness, one small "yes" at a time. And when you don't know what comes next, remember—you're not walking alone. The same God who started this work in you will be faithful to complete it.

Because this isn't the end of the journey. It's the beginning of a new one. And with every step, heaven smiles and whispers, *"That's what love looks like in motion."*

Now go refill your mug, lace up your faith, and take that next step—you've got a world to love.

Declaration
Faith in Motion Declaration

A Closing Commitment for the Journey

Lord,

I choose to **LEARN** Your love. Not just with my mind, but with my heart. I've seen that You know me, pursue me, forgive me, and call me Your own.

I choose to **LEAN** into Your love. To worship You with my life, to trust You in surrender, and to listen for Your voice above all others.

I will **LET** You in. Into the hidden places, the fears, the dreams, and the parts of me still being shaped. Heal what's broken, refill what's empty, and renew what's weary.

By Your strength, I will **LIVE** my faith out loud. One step at a time, one act of obedience at a time, believing that You walk beside me in every season.

I will **LIFT** others the way You have lifted me. Serving with humility, loving with compassion, and seeing people through Your eyes, not my own.

And I will **LIGHT** the way for others to find You. Shining Your love in dark places, carrying Your hope into the world, and keeping my faith in motion until the race is done.

This is my declaration:

To love You fully and completely.
To love others deeply and selflessly.
And to walk faithfully, day by day.

AMEN.

Additional Journal & Notes

Additional Journal & Notes

Additional Journal & Notes

Additional Journal & Notes

About the Author

Lori Joy Bell is a wife, mom, writer, and follower of Jesus whose deepest desire is to love God and love her neighbor well. She is the founder of **Faith in Motion Outreach**, a movement that helps others live out their faith—not just in belief, but in action. Through kind words, small steps, and everyday acts of love, she invites others to walk closely with God and boldly reflect His heart to the world.

Lori isn't a Bible scholar or ministry leader. She's a fellow traveler on the path of faith learning, growing, and trusting Jesus with each step. Her prayer is that as you read, you will not only encounter the love of Christ but also discover fresh courage to put your *Faith in Motion*.

She is also the author of:

- *Faith in Motion: The Heart Behind the Steps*
- *Walking the Beatitude Journey* (Growth Guide)
- *Faith in Motion: Walking with God, Loving Others* (Devotional)
- *Faith in Motion: Shine Your Light* (Devotional)
- *Faith in Motion: Speaking Truth in Love* (Devotional)
- *Faith in Motion: Walking in the Gap* (Devotional)
- *From Word to Walk: Living Out Words That Shape Our Faith* (Growth Guide)
- *Walk in the Spirit: Living Out the Fruit of the Spirit* (Growth Guide)
- *The Armor of God: Strength for the Battle Power for the Walk* (Devotional)
- *The Path to Bethlehem* (Devotional)

To explore these and other books, devotionals, and growth guides, visit **www.faithinmotionoutreach.com**.

Made in the USA
Middletown, DE
22 November 2025